SIX ESSAYS IN HANSEATIC HISTORY

GW00566837

Further details of Poppyland Publishing titles can be found at
www.poppyland.co.uk
*where clicking on the 'Support and Resources' button
will lead to pages specially compiled to support this book
Join us for more Norfolk and Suffolk stories and background at*
www.facebook.com/poppylandpublishing
and follow **@poppylandpub**

Six Essays in Hanseatic History

Brian Ayers
Pamela Cawthorne
Matthew Champion
Andrew Hoyle
David Nicolle
Paul Richards

POPPYLAND
PUBLISHING

First published 2017 by Poppyland Publishing, Cromer, NR27 9AN
www.poppyland.co.uk
ISBN 978-1-909796-33-1
Designed and typeset in 12 on 14.4 pt Gilgamesh
Printed by Lightning Source

Picture credits:
 Archaeological Project Services 46
 Archäologische Landesmuseum 73
 Armand Colin, Paris 109
 Ayers, Brian 16, 19
 Cambridge University Press 49
 Creative Commons BY-SA 2.0 Richard Humphrey 100, Diego Delso, delsophoto 91
 Creative Commons 10
 Elfleet, Kevin 7
 Landeshauptarchiv 75
 Lincolnshire Medieval Graffiti Survey 60
 Marsden, Bill/Humber Archaeology Partnership 18
 Nicolle, David 76, 78, 79, 80, 83, 85
 Norfolk Medieval Graffiti Survey 62, 63, 65, 67, 79
 Poppyland Publishing Front cover
 Richards, Paul 114, 124
 Wikimedia Commons 90, 97, 98, 107
 Wikipedia 103, 105

Front cover picture: The *Lisa von Lübeck* is a representation of a 15th century caravel. In the picture she is making her way up the channel to Lynn, 30th July 2009.

Contents

Foreword

In 2015 King's Lynn celebrated 10 years as a member of the New Hanseatic League which embraces today 187 towns across 16 European countries. During International Hanse Day in May 2015 a History & Archaeology Symposium [HAS] was organised by a local group representing the Hanseatic Club, Marriott's Warehouse Trust, True's Yard Fisherfolk Museum and the King's Lynn Town Guides. Four guest lecturers addressed full audiences on Hanseatic History and Archaeology at Marriott's Warehouse, by the Great Ouse, where the Kamper Kogge (a replica of a Dutch 14th century ship) was moored.

King's Lynn was a significant trading partner of the German Hanseatic towns, from the 13th to the early 16th centuries, and has played a forward role in the New Hanseatic League since 2005. Boston became a member in 2015. This Lincolnshire port on the Wash shares our Hanseatic heritage and features in the book.

To allow more people to access the proceedings of the 2015 HAS Symposium, it was decided to seek the publication of the four lectures. Unavoidable delays in completing this book project have at least enabled us to include two more lectures springing from the HAS Symposium in May 2016.

I would like to thank the other five authors for supporting HAS by spending valuable time in the preparation of their lectures for publication. The book would not have been possible without the collaboration of Poppyland Publishing and I am grateful to Peter Stibbons for his interest. I also appreciate the help given by the HAS committee and to Rebecca Rees above all for her pivotal role in the project.

We trust 'Six Essays in Hanseatic History' will make a good contribution to Hanseatic and Regional History and reach new audiences.

Dr Paul Richards FSA, DL
HAS Chairman
May 2017

The Kamper Kogge moored alongside at King's Lynn, May 2015.

About the Authors

Brian Ayers BA, FSA, FRSA, CIfA is a Research Fellow and Honorary Senior Lecturer at the University of East Anglia. He was Assistant Head of Museums & County Archaeologist for Norfolk until 2008. He is a Fellow of the Society of Antiquaries of London and of the Royal Society of Arts. Brian has published numerous papers, principally concerning urban archaeology. He is the author of an archaeological history of the city of Norwich and of The German Ocean: Medieval Europe around the North Sea.

Dr Pamela Cawthorne has degrees in Politics, Economics and Development Studies. From 1974-1979 she worked in Vienna at the United Nations Industrial Development Organisation (UNIDO) and the United Nations Relief and Works Agency for Palestine Refugees (UNRWA). She resumed academic research at Bath University in 1980 and began a PhD on economic development in south India at the Open University in 1985. She took up a lectureship in Political Economy at the University of Sydney from 1994-2008. She now lives partly in Boston – the town where she grew up – and Sydney. She began serious work on Boston's medieval economic history in 2012 when she also joined the re-formed Boston History Project and assisted Boston Borough Council in its application to join the New Hanse (Die Hanse) in 2015.

Matthew Champion studied for an MA at the University of East Anglia, and is now a full-time freelance archaeologist and historian. He is also project director of the Norfolk and Suffolk Medieval Graffiti Survey; a multi award winning community project. Matthew is a Fellow of the Society of Antiquaries of London and the author of Medieval Graffiti: The Lost Voices of England's Churches.

Dr David Nicolle worked for BBC Television News from 1963 to 1967, before transferring to the BBC Arabic Service, where he worked until 1971. In 1972 he returned to university, eventually receiving a PhD from Edinburgh University. He lectured in art history at Yarmouk University, Jordan from 1983 to 1987. David is a Visiting Research Fellow at the Institute of Medieval Studies, Nottingham University and has over one hundred books to his name.

Andrew Hoyle studied Medieval History at the University of London. He is a member of Boston Hanse Group, The History of Boston Project, Boston Preservation Trust, Boston Heritage Forum, and the Lincolnshire Society for History and Archaeology. He is a former member of Boston Parish Library Committee.

Dr Paul Richards was born and bred in King's Lynn. He studied for both BA and PhD degrees in History and taught in further and higher education for the College of West Anglia and the Open University. Paul was a borough councillor (King's Lynn and West Norfolk) and Mayor (1998-2000) before becoming an Honorary Alderman and Borough Freeman. Paul is a Fellow of the Society of Antiquaries (London) and a Deputy Lieutenant of Norfolk.

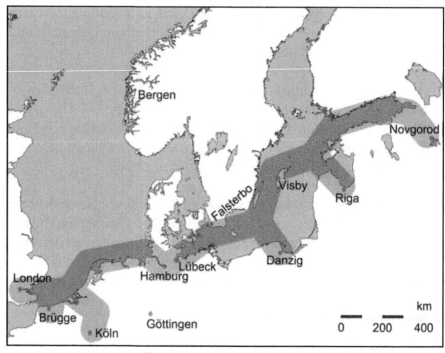

The main Hanseatic trade route.

Archaeological evidence for the material culture of the Hanseatic World

Brian Ayers

This short paper — an edited version of one delivered in King's Lynn in May 2015 — is an attempt to explore briefly the manner in which archaeologists are seeking to understand the development of the Hanseatic World in the Middle Ages. It is not a chronological summary of what happened around the North Sea basin in the medieval period; rather it is a rapid overview of some of the approaches and discoveries that archaeologists bring to augment historical evidence. An historian once said that archaeology is an expensive way of finding out what one already knows. This could be because historians ask questions which are historically-based and do not necessarily ask the type of questions which archaeology is best at answering. Therefore this paper will try to demonstrate that by looking at the evidence that archaeology can provide, a better understanding of the way things happened in the past may emerge.

Archaeological approaches

There is a range of archaeological material upon which to draw — and this can include documents in order to get a documentary framework — often provided by excavations such as urban projects conducted in cities like Stralsund and Lübeck in northern Germany or by survey and analysis of buildings as has been conducted in locations such as s'Hertogenbosch in The Netherlands. Increasingly, a new range of techniques is also available to enable a better understanding of life and society in the Middle Ages. Two such techniques are DNA analysis and isotope analysis. With regards to DNA, only recently the finding of Richard lll under a car park in Leicester has generally been confirmed by DNA linkage between the skeleton and a distant descendant, while DNA analysis of the teeth of Black Death victims excavated at Charterhouse in London has located traces of the *Yersinia pestis* bacterium linked to both pneumonic and bubonic plague. Isotope analysis, based on the principle that the strontium isotope which is taken up in water tends to linger in the teeth of an individual, means that it becomes possible to isolate where somebody had been brought up in the past, aiding studies of migration (in this regard, it has been suggested that with the increased consumption of bottled water today this technique will not be available to archaeologists in the future).

Two local Norfolk examples illustrates how these techniques aid understanding: at Castle Mall in Norwich, excavation uncovered burials, one of which yielded some mitochondrial DNA which was Romany, that is gypsy, dating to the 11th century. The earliest documentary reference for gypsies coming into Britain is from the 16th century and yet here was evidence for one such individual in Norwich in the 11th century. This person almost certainly arrived via Scandinavia, probably from the area of Byzantium, travelling up the Russian rivers, through the Baltic with Anglo-Scandinavian traders and thus to the east of England. Similarly, two other burials were located and here isotope analysis of the teeth indicated that the individuals concerned had been brought up in Orkney. These were people born in Orkney and presumably in later life traded down the east coast before dying and being buried in Norwich. Such information is enabling a much greater awareness of the manner in which people moved around in past societies.

This paper is concerned with the North Sea basin and it is worth drawing attention here to a slightly unusual map, published recently by Tom Williamson, in a volume entitled *East Anglia and the Medieval North Sea World* (2012). The map is of the North Sea but it is upside down or rather, because there is no 'correct' direction in which to view the world, it has south at the top and north at the bottom. This simple reversal of the typical manner of looking at cartographic representation of the region immediately subverts the tyranny of the map. Maps really can be tyrannous. They fossilise ways of seeing and thus ways of thinking. A particular Norfolk problem is countering the notion that 'it is so far away' when it is not 'far away' at all. It merely appears that way when presented as a bump on the side of England. If one turns the map on its side, Norfolk is directly facing Amsterdam and Antwerp, and it is at the centre of what was going on five hundred years ago. Turn it upside down and what one sees immediately is that the North Sea is effectively a great lake, with the countries of England, Scotland, Denmark, Netherlands, the Low Countries and Germany as lakeside communities, perceived as neighbours in contact with one another. Once the map reverts to its 'normal' orientation, the North Sea spreads out into the North Atlantic. It takes on the appearance of a great arm of this huge area but in reality it is quite a small lake compared to the oceans, encouraging trade and contact.

The range of such trade can be seen from information gathered in Hull, amalgamating documentary and ceramic evidence to show the reach of this one port between 1200 and 1700. Mercantile contact extended from Iceland to Bordeaux (and beyond to Spain and Italy), and eastward into the Baltic. It was trade facilitated by technological innovation, notably through the development of deep sea trading craft which could take bulk goods relatively safely across the North Sea. The classic vessel was the Hanseatic cog which began its existence in the 12th century with heavy use thereafter in the 13th, 14th and 15th centuries. Until 50 years ago these ships were generally not that well known. There had been the occasional excavated example, notably in the harbour at Riga in 1939 when a well-preserved cog was located in the harbour and lifted, only to be largely destroyed in the Second World War (the keel of the vessel survives).

It was not until 1962 that an almost intact cog was uncovered, that now known as the Bremen Cog (a replica of which visited King's Lynn in 2004). This extraordinary vessel was found downstream of Bremen, in the river Weser; it appears that she was under construction, probably in a shipyard in Bremen, when lost. She had been completed but not fitted out and broke free of her moorings (presumably in a storm) and drifted downstream, getting stuck on a sandbank, keeling over and sinking. In a similar manner to the lost 16th-century warship the *Mary Rose*, which also keeled over, one side of the vessel was extremely well-preserved and the other less so. She was lifted and is now the centrepiece of the Deutsche Schiffahrtsmuseum Museum in Bremerhaven and probably one of the best surviving cogs anywhere.

Flat-bottomed, carvel-built at the very base, and then clinker-built above with great stem and stern posts, cogs were robust ships. Two more were discovered during the extension of the harbour in Antwerp in 2000, regrettably without any prior archaeological investigation although there is now a large research project being undertaken by the University at Antwerp into the vessels, with some interesting results. For instance examination of the caulking of one of the ships is very informative. The vessel obviously moved around the North and Baltic Seas, every now and then needing to have its caulking renewed. Moss inserted to prevent leaking survives and can be traced to its source so that one can get some idea of the trading patterns of the ship from the caulking of the vessel itself.

Resources and Commodities

These vessels, the people who crewed them, the people who funded them and sent them out, were exploiting a range of natural resources all around the North Sea and the Baltic and turning those into commodities. Examples of important traded resources were fish, wool from England, timber from the Baltic (particularly in the area of Poland), and iron ore from Sweden. The commodities which were created from these raw materials included fresh, dried and salted cod (an extensive trade), cloth (firstly in the Low Countries and increasingly in England) and wine (from the Rhineland).

The implications of this are interesting because it is possible in some instances to trace archaeologically how people traded certain commodities. The marketing of fish is a good example. The number of people living from the end of the 11th century onwards increased very dramatically. Larger, more densely-populated urban areas became established with greater requirements for protein. A good source of protein is fish. An economical way to get the fish to such urban populations is to dry them or salt them. And thus the trade in salt became very important. There are two or three areas where sufficient quantities of salt could be produced. Coastal salterns could burn it from brine deposits and considerable evidence of that process survives around the North Sea: in the area of the Wash, as waste deposits in the so-called Red Hills of Essex, and on the Low Countries' coast. However, it was a time-consuming process, costly and produced an inferior quality salt. Expensive bay salt could be sourced from the Bay of Biscay but that increased costs significantly.

The best location for good quality salt at an economical price was Lüneburg in North Germany where there was a huge area of brine salt and where enormous quantities were produced throughout the Middle Ages. The early 17th-century prospect by Braun and Hogenberg illustrated the saltworks, an area of 54 huts, each hut containing four great lead brine pans. Unfortunately, Lüneburg is land-based, isolated from the Baltic and the northern North Sea where its salt was needed. In order to transport the salt north, it had first to reach Lübeck, the great Hanseatic distribution centre. An early route was that of the *Salzweg*, a 70 or 80 km road running north of Lüneburg, but it was one which involved inclines, was subject to banditry and ensuing problems of continuity of supply. Accordingly, in the 1290s, the Germans built a canal, the *Stecknitzkanal*, the first summit level canal with locks in Europe. The canal is little-known because, in the mid-19th century, the length of it was essentially followed by the Trave-Elbe canal which widened and deepened the 13th century canal for the larger 19th century craft. Recently, however, the University of Kiel has undertaken a major survey of the canal and has been able to isolate where the medieval locks were situated. Using a combination of archaeological survey and hydrography it has been possible to determine that where the obviously 19th-century *Palmschleuse* lock now exists, there must also have been a medieval chamber lock. Salt boats were thus able to reach Lübeck, emerging into the river Trave. The port on the Trave lay in two parts, either side of the sole bridge by the great gate, the Holstentor. Downstream of that bridge was the sea port with the inland port upstream. At this latter the salt barges unloaded their cargoes from Lüneburg ready for trans-shipment;

17th -century salt warehouses still stand immediately upstream of the Holstentor on the river's edge.

Salt warehouses in Lübeck.

The salt went first to Falsterbo, then ultimately to Bergen. Falsterbo is in south-western Sweden, just south of Malmö where there is a great curving bay and where a huge herring market was held every year in the 13th and 14th centuries (the herring used to shoal in massive numbers in the Öresund between Denmark and Sweden). Merchants of Lübeck, Hamburg and other German towns met at Falsterbo and the adjacent village of Skanör, many of them leaving incised graffiti of their merchants' marks on the oak door of Skanör church.

German merchants also visited - and lived in - Bryggen (or Bergen) in Norway. The name Bryggen almost certainly meant wharf, the German wharf at Bergen. Waterfront buildings of the 17th century survive but it has been demonstrated archaeologically that these stand on the footprints of structures established there in the 12th century. This was a German enclave where the Germans controlled the trade, principally salting and drying fish in Bergen which could then be shipped to the great urban centres of north-western Europe - Lübeck itself, Hamburg, Bremen, Antwerp, Amsterdam, Mechelen, York, King's Lynn, Norwich, and London.

Archaeological work over the last 40 years or so has now produced a range of fishbone material which is helping to increase understanding about this trade in fish, and is thus providing a much greater awareness of the commercial activity at this period. Large assemblages of such bone, collected and stored from the 1970s onward, has enabled James Barrett of the University of Cambridge, working with other scholars (notably in Flanders), to undertake isotopic analysis of the jaw bones of fish. In so doing, he and his colleagues have been able to determine where those fish were spawned and where they were caught. This in turn means that, from the fishbone assemblages located in excavations of places such as York, Norwich, London, Ghent and Mechelen, it is possible to explore both the provenance and the distribution of fish.

The results are remarkable. Initially, in the 9th — 10th centuries, in England all the fish was derived from the southern North Sea, but by the 13th and 14th centuries, London was sourcing 50% of its cod from the northern North Sea. The implications are firstly that, with the available technology at the time, the southern North Sea had already been over-fished, so it could be argued that the origins of the modern fishing crisis date back to the 13th century. Secondly, a sophisticated trading economy was already in place at this period so that it was worthwhile for merchants to source fish from the northern North Sea and bring it south to urban populations. Further new discoveries remain possible; DNA testing on cod bones can also be undertaken helping to isolate individual shoals within the northern North Sea. Soon therefore, where now for instance it can be stated that a sample of fish came from somewhere off Orkney, somewhere off Norway and somewhere off Iceland, in the future it should be possible to determine that they were fished off Aberdeen, or Bergen or Reykjavik and brought down to London. Archaeology will then be able to identify the likely micro trade that was being pursued.

Tabulation of the archaeological fishbone assemblages illustrates the enormous rise in the consumption of fish in the central Middle Ages although there was something of a dip in the middle of the 14th century, which was presumably an effect of the Black Death. Towns were

also importing fresh fish – one can differentiate between fresh and salted or dried specimens because fresh fish still had their heads, whereas dried and salted fish had to have the head removed before shipping. Fresh fish was stored as can be seen from evidence in Hull. Late 15th-century casks made of Baltic timber uncovered by excavation in Hull were almost certainly used for storing live fish.

Casks of Baltic oak, possibly for storing live fish, found at Blaydes Staith, Hull.

Urban Topographical Change

The use of deep drafted trading vessels impacted upon the urban topography of ports. A great ship such as the Bremen Cog needed to have a wharf against which to berth and then unload. Rivers with a significant tidal rise and fall, as in London, King's Lynn or Hull, required increasingly sophisticated timber wharf revetments to enable the ever-larger shipping to dock. In consequence, sophisticated timber technologies developed at estuarine waterfronts as seen at the extensive excavation at Trig Lane in London. Such great revetments also brought changes in the urban topography because, as structures were extended deeper and deeper into the water, so riverbanks had to be built up in order to constrain the water within the river channels into smaller areas. This in turn increased the pressure from the water and also increased the pressure from the land where the dumping of material behind the revetments itself became deeper and deeper. Timber technology therefore needed to become more sophisticated. The topographical impact is evident in King's Lynn where the lines of both King Street and Queen Street effectively reflect the original wharf alignments; most of the land west of these streets, between them and the river Ouse, consists of infilled ground.

The riverward growth in King's Lynn was essentially accidental topographical change. In contrast, there is evidence from Lübeck where topographical change, extending part of the city into the river Trave, was a result of quite deliberate topographical manipulation. Lübeck had a problem; as it grew, roughly from about 1160 onwards, a very low, marshy embayment near St Peter's church, occupying a large area, could not be used. Archaeological work in the form of a series of keyhole excavations undertaken beneath the standing buildings of Große Petersgrube discovered 13th-century evidence for considered, deliberate deposition of material over a period of about 40 years in order to level up this entire area so that it could then be developed

Große Petersgrube, Lübeck.

as a new area of the town.   This action was marked by the building of timber caissons which then had infilling placed within and around them.   This was not happenstance development, piecemeal, one property by another, but a corporate endeavour. It appears, moreover, to be a completely undocumented action yet clearly the product of a sophisticated urban society with sufficient capital and political ability to enable this enormous operation to take place.   Thus is archaeology helping to expand understanding of the socio-political and economic situation in some of the greater towns of medieval north-western Europe.

Countryside – Landscape and Resources

Landscape manipulation can also be seen in the countryside. As an example, around Terrington St Clement in west Norfolk there is evidence for the medieval construction of a range of sea dykes in order to protect the region, to assist with drainage, and to improve the agriculture of the area. Similar activity took place on the other side of the North Sea as well. At Westergo in Friesland, consolidation of the coastal margin here consisted initially of the construction of a series of *terpen*, small dwelling mounds, on which to build a single house. Often established in rows, the *terpen* would gradually become linked together and would form a primitive dyke system. Drainage could then start to reclaim the land. Such initiatives at an individual level were also adopted more corporately, with archaeological investigation beginning to uncover evidence for such corporate activity, particularly in the Low Countries. Monasteries moved into marginal lands and drained the areas in order to make them secure for occupation, notably for agriculture and therefore for revenue generation. At Boudelo in Flanders, a monastic site, the use of electro-magnetic induction as part of an extensive landscape survey revealed a whole series of drainage and buried dyke systems. This was followed by targeted excavation to establish a range of chronologies.

The countryside obviously provided resources to the towns of northern Europe. Recent excavation within the 'foundation quarter' of Lübeck has uncovered waterlogged deposits which preserved great timbers as well as much leather and other organic material, all products of the countryside. The earliest buildings excavated were of timber and, so as to construct them and others like them elsewhere, the timber itself needed to be sourced. Dendro-provenancing of such buildings across northern Europe suggests that much timber was derived from the Polish forests and from the forests of the Baltic states, especially Latvia and Lithuania. Much of the timber trade was associated with Riga, with a great deal of Riga timber being imported to King's Lynn (so much so that it is documented as 'Righolt', the name Riga thus becoming the term for the wood itself). Large quantities of wood were also exported through Danzig (now Gdańsk) and, in order to get the timber out of these forests, a canal, once again, was built (this time towards the end of the 14th century – c.1390-1400). This piece of infrastructure linked rivers together so that, from the forests around Kaunus, timber could be brought to Danzig and thus exported both to towns along the Baltic and to others around the North Sea as well. Analysis of relatively small structures, such as herring barrels used to line a cesspit in Einbeck, Germany, demonstrate the widespread application of Baltic oak.

Stone was another traded commodity. A survey undertaken in Norfolk by Andrew Rogerson and Steven Ashley examined every church in the county in order to inspect the fabric for the re-use of lava quern stones derived from the Niedermendig region of the Rhineland. Incidence and numbers were plotted and the plotting results are interesting. The stones proved to be most numerous in the river valleys, presumably because of the ease of carriage by river, but they occur most frequently in the eastern river valleys, and to some extent in the north, with very little around King's Lynn. This makes sense, because the trade of Norwich and Great Yarmouth was aimed directly across the North Sea and into the Rhineland basin. King's Lynn's trade was more aligned with the Baltic.

Trade Items and Networks

Smaller artefacts, such as cloth seals, are also indicative of contacts. A range of seals is found in Britain including those of foreign manufacture, notably seals associated with high quality Flemish cloth (an example is a 14th-century seal for a Brabant cloth from Mechelen in Flanders found at Swan Lane in London). Tracing the movement of people is also occasionally possible with individual finds. A mould for the manufacture of pilgrim badges was discovered in an archaeological survey undertaken in Norwich at the site of the arts cinema called Cinema City. It was found to be the very mould in which was cast an intact pilgrim badge, itself located on the Thames foreshore at London Bridge in 1899. The badge depicts the Annunciation of the Virgin and was from Walsingham. It is possible therefore to envisage an individual from London taking ship up the east coast, perhaps to one of the Glaven ports such as Cley or Wiveton, or to Lynn, landing at the Purfleet which is known to have handled pilgrims. This person would then have proceeded overland to Walsingham, purchased a pilgrim badge there, returned to the Norfolk port, taken ship to London, got off the ship at London Bridge perhaps with the souvenir pilgrim badge attached to a hat from which it became detached, and lost the badge when it fell into the river.

Even more interestingly, when this particular artefact was analysed, it was plain that it was made by the same craftsperson who was making badges for the shrine of St Thomas Becket at Canterbury. One is tempted to think that, in the Middle Ages with shrines all over the country, local craftspeople would be making pilgrim badges for local shrines - Canterbury artisans manufacturing Thomas Becket badges and Walsingham artisans the badges of Our Lady. The Cinema City discovery, however, seems to imply that, on the contrary, major centres such as Norwich were not only making pilgrim badges for a relatively local shrine such as Walsingham, but badges for Canterbury as well. Thus archaeology illustrates the probability of a more sophisticated and centralised manufacturing economy with a web of trading networks.

Trade networks of the 11th century have been examined by Søren Sindbæk, formerly of the University of York and now at the University of Aarhus. He has sought artefacts which can be typologically tied to a place, and then has seen where else they have been found. In this way he can suggest trade networks and their relative importance one to another and of individual centres. Thus, at this period, Hedeby near Schleswig, which ultimately gave way to Lübeck, was the centre from which much radiated.

For the later period of the high Middle Ages, apart from major German towns such as Bremen, Hamburg and Lübeck, substantial

Hanseatic *kontors* at Novgorod, Bergen, Bruges and London were established. Bruges is particularly of interest as one of these great nodal points of commercial activity. The extraordinary survival of its medieval urban environment enables the manner in which trade developed to be observed. Bruges contained numerous merchants who needed capital and, more to the point, banks with a system of trust and exchange to enable them to buy and sell goods. Thus early banks were set up in the city by Italian merchants, grouped around the square of Beursplein. Originally they were housed in one building, the Huis Ter Beurze (which still exists) belonging to the Terbeurs family but soon the Italians set up their own houses, so that, in the same square, were the Genovese, the Venetians and the Florentines (two of whose buildings also survive). The Terbeurs family decorated their house with its coat of arms (three money bags on a shield) and probably gave its name to the word Bourse, used across Europe for Stock Exchange.

Archaeology and Medieval Culture

The historic environment assists understanding of commercial organisation and urban settlements elsewhere as well. At Dragon Hall in Norwich, where there is a great warehouse complex dateable to 1427, it has been possible through archaeology and the study of the fabric and documents to suggest the manner in which that complex operated under the ownership of a cloth merchant called Robert Toppes. Even lost terrestrial archaeology can be examined, as at Dunwich in Suffolk where Oxford Archaeology has been undertaking an extraordinary underwater survey. Dunwich is known to have contained seven churches, four monasteries and a great guildhall, all lost under the North Sea. Submarine archaeological survey has been able to identify, through a whole range of sonar and other techniques, the location of various churches which fell into the sea but fell in large chunks, and settled on the sea bed. Early plans of Dunwich have been rectified digitally vis à vis the individual monuments and, with these key points, it becomes possible to suggest a reconstructed layout of the town itself.

Lost art has been discovered through archaeological excavation. Thirteenth-century tombs in the Church of Our Lady in Bruges were uncovered, brick-lined vaults containing coffins. Removal of the coffins revealed extraordinary paintings on the inside of the tomb, of censing angels, Christ and the Virgin and other images. As well as Bruges, such paintings are now also known from excavations in Antwerp.

Archaeology can explore the transmission of technologies. The use of brick is one such innovation, as in 1180 at Lübeck where a great defensive tower was built in the material. Some 80 years later, around 1260, a large cloth hall was built of brick in Flanders. Eventually, early in the 14th century, the east end and transepts of Holy Trinity church, Hull, were constructed in brick as were the town defences there. The use of brick in England became more common thereafter, such as the artillery defensive work known as the Cow Tower in Norwich, which was constructed in 1398-1399.

Archaeological analysis can even suggest the movement of ideas. The *Britons Arms*, on Elm Hill, Norwich, is now known after recent conservation to date from about 1400-1420 because the roof is made of Baltic oak of that period. It was a small building within which women were living in the middle of the 15th century as a community but not as nuns. Examination of the fabric of the building has shown that it was originally established as a series of small rooms with little lamp niches, accessed by an external stairway to the first floor level, with the main door at first floor level going directly out to the churchyard which is higher up the hill. Thus the structure was linked to St Peter Hungate church. The possibility is that this building housed not a nunnery but something akin to a beguinage. These institutions were established in the Low Countries in the medieval period and tended to consist of women who were either spinsters with their own money, or widows with their own income, living in a community and looking after themselves. There is no documentary evidence that such communities existed in Britain but Norwich is the nearest city in England to the Low Countries and therefore may have drawn cultural inspiration from there for the creation of an establishment similar to the movement on the continent.

It has been suggested that the study of ceramics can be used to identify cultural signatures. In Kalmar, in southern Sweden, drainage of the harbour in the 1930s led to the discovery of very large quantities of ceramics, many from Germany and the Low Countries, with a probable destination being the known medieval German *émigré* community. However, such ceramics also reached the hinterland of Kalmar, thus serving the local Swedish population as well.   Similarly, English ceramics crossed the North Sea to continental Europe. A fragment of a Scarborough ware knight jug was recently found in Lüneburg, and some 80% of the medieval pottery found in Bergen seems to have been made in Pott Row, Grimston, near King's Lynn (Norway was effectively aceramic at this period with great quantities therefore imported from eastern England).   However, there were limits to cultural movement. In Novgorod, the great *kontor* in Russia, the river effectively divided the German enclave where the market was, from that of the Russians on the other bank, although there was also a small German area near the Kremlin.   The ceramic finds from excavations in Novgorod all derive from the German enclave, the Russians using wooden vessels, not ceramics. Despite their close physical proximity, a form of Slavic/ Germanic cultural divide persisted throughout the Middle Ages.

Hanseatic Europe as evidenced by archaeology was a managed landscape with a developing urban-focussed economy, a technologically innovative Europe, and one increasingly maximising the natural resources available. Thus the title of this lecture — Cities, Cogs and Commerce.

Author's Note: This text is an edited version of the transcript of a lecture given in King's Lynn during 'Hanse Weekend' in May 2015. Full references to the excavations and surveys mentioned are provided in the lecturer's book *The German Ocean: Medieval Europe around the North Sea* (2016).

Brian Ayers
School of History
University of East Anglia
Norwich NR4 7TJ

Medieval Boston and the German Hanse [c.1250-1474]

Dr Pamela M. Cawthorne, Boston History Project

Boston Port and Its Medieval Fair: A Most Cosmopolitan Town

Boston faced the right direction, along with other ports strung out along the east coast. If England during the twelfth and thirteenth centuries was Queen of Wool, Flanders on the opposite coast was King of Cloth. Port towns on the east coast became important headports or coastal outlets (hence also transhipment points for both imports and exports) for wealthy towns further inland: Boston outport[1] for the city of Lincoln; Kingston-upon-Hull headport to Beverley and York; Lynn and Yarmouth were not far from Bury St Edmunds (the site of an important fair) nor from Cambridge and Norwich; Ipswich lay close to Colchester and all with their woolly hinterlands.[2]

---

1   Boston served as an 'outport' for Lincoln but also served as the 'headport' between Hull and Lynn. The term 'headport' means the town was a chief port of a customs jurisdiction. Thanks to Rigby, communication August 2016. Also see Kowaleski (2000) Map 19.1 of England's Customs Headports, p. 473 in Palliser.

2   The diversity and quality of English wool during these centuries was unmatched anywhere else in Europe and was at its peak in the early fourteenth century. This is not to suggest England was not producing cloth of its own, nor that there were not other wool growers. But England did not export much cloth until the pattern and structure of trade towards cloth and away from wool began, slowly and over a long period during the mid fourteenth century. For a detailed breakdown of the exports of wool and cloth for all the east coast port towns at this period, see Carus-Wilson and Coleman (1963).

Boston's port was riverine, which meant that although it was somewhat protected from the sea, it was always subject to silting. But to have a port — the port was then the banks of the river Witham in the centre of the town - meant that waterfront activity resulted in what could be called valuable infrastructural development: warehouses, cellars, cranes and weigh-beams[3] yielding rents or fees. Trade expanded so much that by the early fifteenth century, a whole host of 'port and shore duties for the use of [those] facilities, included anchorage, ballastage, bushellage, cranage, keelage and towage.. [levied].. on incoming and departing ships, goods and merchants'.[4] Boston's early wealth was closely tied to its status as a port. Table (a) ranks the top eight towns by the beginning of the thirteenth century and indicates the importance of three east coast port town, including Boston, relative to London.

Table (a): the fifteenth impost of 1203-1204, levied on all imports and exports showing the wealthiest eight trading towns at that time.[5]	
1. London	£836 12s 10d
2. Boston*	£780 15s 3d
3. Southampton	£712 3s 7d
4. Lincoln	£656 12s 2d
5. Lynn*	£651 11s 11d
6. Hull*	£344 14s 14d
7. York	£175 8s 10d
8. Newcastle	£158 5s 11d

Tables (b) and (c) also convey how towns could be ranked for their importance to England's overseas trade. In addition, Table (c) shows how little of Boston's 'alien' trade overall was left by 1478, as well as with the Hanse specifically due to the Anglo-Hanse war (1468-1474), see section II. During that war, Boston's overseas trade was decimated

3   Gysors (Gisors) Hall in South Square was once the weigh house in Boston built in the first half of the thirteenth century. It was named for a London wool merchant who had been an early tenant. Some original stones remain in the floor of the current building. Gurnham (2014) p. 15.

4   Kowaleski (2000) p. 471 in Palliser. This is before the revenue from customs duties is taken into account, the basis of the data in tables (b) and (c). Also see section II.

5   Lloyd (1977) Table 1 p. 12.

(as was the trade of other east coast port towns) and London's pre-eminent position became thoroughly consolidated relative to all other east coast port towns by the end of the fifteenth century, see Table (b). London controlled '...roughly 17% of the country's overseas trade at the beginning of the thirteenth century and approximately 61% by the end of the fifteenth'.[6] Together these three tables indicate what happened to Boston's medieval trading economy between the thirteenth and fifteenth centuries. Carus-Wilson[7] called this a 'wheel of fortune' which carried Boston to dizzy heights, only to bring it low again.

Table (b): the relative importance of London and three east coast headports in overseas trade using the fifteenth and customs data (out of 12 port towns)[8]			
Customs Headport	1203-1204 % value (fifteenth)	Customs Headport	1478-1482 % value (customs)
1. Boston (+ Lincoln)	29.0%	1. London	60.9%
2. London	16.9%	7. Boston	2.8%
3. Hull	15.4%	5. Hull	4.4%
5. Lynn	13.1%	11. Lynn	0.7%

Table (c): the relative importance of London and three east coast headports in alien overseas trade using customs data (out of 15 port towns)				
Customs Headport	% of total alien trade 1324-1329	Customs Headport	% of total alien trade 1478-1482	% of Hanse in alien trade 1478-1482
1. London	40.2%	1. London	65.4%	86.4%
2. Boston	30.7%	7. Lynn	1.1%	1.6%
3. Hull	6.3%	4. Hull	3.5%	6.8%
4. Lynn	5.2%	8. Boston	0.8%	1.6%

6   Kowaleski (2000) p. 485 in Palliser.

7   Carus Wilson (1962-63) p. 182.

8   Kowaleski (2000) pp. 467-94 in Palliser Tables (b) and (c) above are based on Kowaleski's Table 19.1, p. 477 and Table 19.4 p. 482, reconstructed to produce the rankings. In table (b) she has added Lincoln data to Boston and I am grateful to Rigby for pointing this out.

Boston's fair also aided and abetted the town's early mercantile success.[9] That Boston, very early on,[10] had such a fair surely made it a doubly useful port destination for overseas merchants. European merchants were accustomed to such fairs, long known in Champagne and in Flanders 'where the Counts of Flanders in Ypres, Lille, Messen and Torhout established the first fairs in northern Europe as early as the beginning of the twelfth century'.[11] 'Alien' merchants in England were restricted in their buying and selling but they were allowed to trade at annual fairs which functioned then as specialised, infrequently held, markets. The Great Fairs (as they were known) were, in effect, 'international trading emporia' where an extraordinary variety of highly valuable, imported commodities — wine, furs, hawks, spices, wax, amber, honey and cloth — amongst much else, could be bought and sold for the conspicuous consumers of the time: the church and the monasteries, the feudal aristocracy and the king.[12]

But these fairs also served as wholesale outlets for wool allowing bulk sales and purchases by English as well as alien merchants. Much of the wool sold to exporters, as well as settlements for sales, were made at the Great Fairs of which the annual fair of Boston was probably the most important.[13] The church itself in the form of the monasteries, especially the Benedictines and the Cistercians, soon took advantage of the growing wool trade and, alongside other merchants, had their own houses and warehouses in towns such as Boston to more easily transact business.[14]

9 Rigby (2017) has the first detailed exploration of this period of Boston's medieval economy.

10 Boston's fair was first mentioned in 'Count Alan's charter to St. Mary's Abbey by Count Stephen of Brittany Charter in the period 1125 and 1135 when the monks were given the right to take their profits in the time of the fair both in and out of the churchyard [St. Botolphs] at Boston' Rigby (2012) pp. 6-28 in Badham and Cockerham. Before 1218 the fair lasted a week from 17-24th June, but was gradually extended and it was July 26th when the fair was deliberately set on fire in 1288 — meaning the fair by then had lasted more than five weeks. For a detailed account of the fire see Summerson (2014) pp. 146-165 in Barron and Sutton.

11 Hammel-Kiesow (2015) p. 35.

12 Miller and Hatcher (1995) p.170.

13 For a recent account of the importance of wool and overseas trade to Boston's early economy see Rigby (2012) pp. 10-11.

14 See Harden (1978) Fig. 4 'Religious houses in England with properties in Boston', p. 8. Fountains Lane is still a small alleyway just off Wormgate behind St. Botolph's church named for Fountains Abbey. Although the monasteries were important, this is not to suggest that they dominated wool production.

Fairs, like markets - if much more intermittently - offered additional lucrative sources of revenue: rent from stalls; rents for accommodation; various tolls; payments for grazing animals and last but not least profits from the courts that had to be held to manage disputes of one kind or another. By 1200, gross returns[15] from the Boston fair 'often reached 100 pounds or more.'[16]

Moore writes[17] '[it is] no coincidence that all [England's] major fairs were, for the most part, located in the towns of east England' and circuits developed which allowed both local and overseas merchants to visit several in any one year. Thus fairs were held in Stamford during Lent; St Ives at Easter; Boston in June; Winchester in September and Northampton in November. King's Lynn too had a fair in late July and cloth from Ypres and Douai in Flanders was sold at Bury St Edmunds in December.

The fairs reached their zenith around the end of the thirteenth century and thereafter began to dwindle in economic importance as the Flemish traders in England became less important and 'as English textiles captured more of the market earlier served by imports.'[18] The decline in England's wool export trade also accelerated largely as a result of the Government imposing heavy export duties to pay for the Hundred Years War with France (1337-1453) and because of fifteenth century bullion policies.[19] How to substitute other economic activity if the port lost ground was an ongoing problem. The fur trade, for example, became concentrated in the centre of London and drew imports where once the king's agents had been despatched far and wide to obtain furs at the Great Fairs including Boston.[20]

Boston did, however, stave off what might otherwise have been a more rapid decline as its connection with the Bergen stockfish and fish oil trade grew to supplant the loss of the wool trade. This was entirely organised by the Hanse who already knew the town well.[21] Those

---

15 That is, income for the honour of Richmond. The actual profits to merchants and others were much greater. Rigby communication, August 2016.

16 Miller and Hatcher (1995) p. 168. Rigby (2017) section 4e.

17 Wedemeyer Moore (1985).

18 Miller and Hatcher (1995) p. 175.

19 Rigby, communication July 2016.

20 See Veale (1966).

21 While 'Low-German' speaking towns were concentrated in a similar region to today's Germany, in the medieval period this formed part of the Holy Roman Empire. As

merchants became known as 'Englandfahrer' and they set up a triangular trading route between Lübeck, Bergen and Boston. The Norwegians needed grain and only the Hanse merchants could provide for that level of demand. Boston was drawn into close co-operation with the Bergen Hanse *kontor*, part of a trade axis involving cloth (out from Boston to Lübeck), grain (from Lübeck to Bergen) and stockfish (from Bergen to Boston).[22] This was the single most important extended contribution the Hanse merchants made to the town c.1370-1470.

The Hanse and Boston

> They [the Hanse] were the most highly privileged group of foreigners in England, and they kept the rich Baltic trade almost entirely in their own hands. Their main centres in England were in London, Boston and Lynn. In these places they were allowed to dwell free from interference in their depots. It was a highly cherished privilege. All other aliens, and the English themselves when they went to Baltic ports, were forced to 'go to host', that is to live in the house and under the supervision of a native merchant: a form of commercial chaperonage that was highly unpopular. The Hanseatic merchants also paid customs at a lighter rate than other aliens. That is why their goods are enumerated separately in the customs accounts.[23]

Northern Europe, in large part due to the mercantile activities of the Hanse, developed a well-connected web of specialised trading routes all along the Baltic coast or beside rivers or simply strategically located for trade. Towns sprang up in their wake — Riga (1201), Rostock (1218); Danzig (1224), Wismar (1229), Stralsund (1234), Elbing (1237); Stettin (1243); Greifswald (1250) and Königsberg (1255).[24] Furs and wax,

merchants from these towns developed their trade networks they colonized the entire Baltic region as far as Novgorod and came to completely dominate trade in Scandinavia. As a result political allegiances were complex which partly accounts for the weakness of the Lübeck Hanse as a central political organization. Member towns looked to their own local politics first. For example, Imperial cities such as Lübeck and Köln owed allegiance to the Emperor; Danzig to the King of Poland, Bremen to its Archbishop; Arnheim to the Duke of Guelders and so on.

22 Burkhardt (2015) p. 144.
23 Haward (1933) p. 172
24 Ewert and Selzer (2015) p. 167.

Dollinger[25] argues, can be seen as a countertrade to the cloth and wool of western Europe. But the Hanse traded in a wide variety of commodities as table (d) shows and grain and timber were just as important. The Hanse came to monopolise all trade in the Baltic region as far east as Novgorod; to control the Skania fisheries in Sweden and to occupy the strategic island of Gotland (Germans had settled there by 1161), as well as establishing the Bergen *kontor* in Norway by the middle of the fourteenth century.

Table (d): origins of the main commodities imported into England from North and Central Europe from a number of Hanse-controlled outposts and elsewhere c. 1150-1500[26]					
Muscovy (Hanse kontor: Novgorod)	Scandinavia, Gotland, Iceland (Hanse kontor Bergen)	The Baltic and Poland	'Germany' (north & mid) (Hanse HQ: Lübeck)	The Low Countries (Hanse kontor Bruges)	France
Furs	Fish, Fish oil, Stockfish, Herring	Grain	Grain	Linen, woolcloth, tapestry	Yellow, blue dye
Honey	Pitch	Timber	Silver, copper, iron, lead	Red dye	Stone, grain
Wax	Timber	Wax	Fustians	Bricks, tiles, pottery	Linen, wool cloth, tapestry
	Iron, copper	Butter	Wine	Butter	Wine
	Potash	Oxen	Salt	[NB Tournai marble]	
	Falcons	Tar, potash	Dairy produce	Glass	
		Linen			
		Amber			

The merchants of these Low German-speaking towns came to form three distinct regions: a western wing (the towns of the Zuider Zee, Westphalia and the Rhine) an eastern wing (the towns of Prussia and Livonia - their

25 Dollinger (1963) pp. 212-302.

26 For an excellent survey of commodities traded in the Baltic during this period see Jahnke (2015) pp. 194-240.

merchants were known as 'Esterlings' or 'Easterlings' in England) and the centre (Saxon and Wendish towns, above all Lübeck).[27] By the fourteenth and fifteenth centuries the Hanse merchants were almost as powerful as their southern Italian counterparts,[28] certainly in England.

Internally, the Hanse, like the Italians, set up partnerships and used intermarriage as a means of cementing business relationships. For example, 'at the beginning of the fifteenth century Hildebrand Veckinchusen carried out commercial transactions with his brothers, his father-in-law, his nephews and his friends in London, Lübeck, Danzig, Riga, Tallinn and Dorpat.' The result was that a merchant in Tallinn could keep an eye on a region that ranged from Novgorod and Central Europe to Bruges, England and Spain.[29]

By 1226, Lübeck had been proclaimed an Imperial Free City of the Holy Roman Empire but the Hanseatic Confederation did not begin to hold regular assemblies or Hanse 'diets' (*Hansetag*) until 1356 which representatives of 'member' towns could attend. But even these were often poorly attended and infrequent and a complete list of constituent members was never published throwing doubt on the usefulness of terms such as 'Hanseatic League' popular in English. Instead, certificates were issued pronouncing that a town was genuinely a member of the Hanse and 'that therefore the citizens of that town, to whom a separate certificate was often given, were entitled to enjoy whatever privileges had been granted to the Hanse in any particular foreign country.'[30] At meetings, matters of common interest such as troublesome nobles or pirates and new members or new *kontore* were discussed but the Lübeck ordinances, or *rezesse* never carried any real mandatory power.

Perhaps not so strangely, it was in the overseas *kontore* where strict rules and regulations were developed along with well-honed forms

27 Postan (1933) p. 95. Dollinger (1963) calls this period of regional groupings of towns with Lübeck in its consolidating role the 'Hanse of the towns'.

28 Although never quite as able or willing to lend to the English Crown.

29 Notes from a visit to the Hanse Museum, Lübeck, May 2015. See also Ewert and Selzer (2015) p. 184 Fig. 5.3 is a diagram of the family network of Hildebrand Veckinchusen showing their trading relationships and geographical diffusion.

30 Salter (1931) p. 98. Dollinger (1963) estimates that there were perhaps 70 active towns at any one time plus approximately 100 others. Perhaps 'amorphous commercial entente' is as good a description as any, see Arnold-Baker (1996). Whether or not the term 'Hanseatic League' is useful, the English towns as foreign 'kontore' could never have been members of it.

of political representation. *Kontor* (the term was not used until the sixteenth century and simply means 'office') describes a combination of warehousing and accommodation, that the Hanse became so adept at setting up. These associations for German merchants abroad were the backbone of Hanseatic trade. Unlike the community of Hanse towns represented in Lübeck, each *kontor* had the legal status of a corporation and each had their own seal. In the case of London and Bruges a two-headed eagle, in Bergen a codfish and in Novgorod the key of St. Peter. All visiting merchants had to present themselves to the authorities of the *kontor*, follow its statutes and lodge there. A *kontor* was set up in Muscovy at Novgorod (1191-92), in Gotland at Visby (1160), later in Bergen, Norway, and Kalmo in Sweden; in Bruges, Flanders and Antwerp and in London. Under Henry II (1157) Cologne had bought the Hall of the Danes which became the House of Cologne merchants (*Gildhalle der Deutschen und des Hansischen Stalhofes*) and under Richard I (1194) Cologne merchants were free to trade throughout England — they had raised money for his ransom. These privileges were later confirmed by King John in return for the maintenance of Bishopsgate. The election of their own aldermen in England, for example (in the London Steelyard, but also in the smaller Steelyards or 'outposts'[31] such as Boston and later Lynn) were the means to ensure that Hanse interests and privileges were both continually pursued and subsequently protected in domestic politics and they became nifty practitioners of '*handelspolitik*'. By the fourteenth century, London's Hanse Steelyard was effectively a 'city within a city'. But above all, the Hanse used their overseas locations both to manage and acquire greater control over supplies of the commodities they traded.

Hanse merchants' trade activity in medieval Boston falls into three main periods. Cologne merchants were in Lincolnshire c. 1150, when they are first mentioned in the early 1200s and when Boston's fair was at its peak.

---

31   Burkhardt (2015) p. 158 distinguishes between the larger *kontore* such as London or Bruges and smaller 'outposts' of which there were around 50, distinct from the larger *kontore* because they were not all permanently manned. He classes Newcastle, Scarborough, Hull, Boston, King's Lynn, Norwich, Yarmouth and Ipswich as such small 'outposts'. But whether this was true of Hull, Boston and Lynn should be further investigated. Lloyd (1991) who remains the *English* authority on the Hanse says there were 12 or 13 small Hanse *kontore* in the towns on the east coast while 'at Boston there had been an organized *kontor* for two or three centuries' (p. 277). He says there is no proof that the Hanse were actually in possession of the building described in section III and Nedkvitne (2014) p. 153 also says that the Hanse Steelyard in Boston was only rented premises, which might make more sense of their laying claim to it at the Treaty of Utrecht settlement in 1474.

They had become well-established in London importing wine. During this period, merchants from many parts of Europe visited the town to trade a huge variety of commodities at the fair: the Hanse did not dominate.

Easterlings (as merchants from Lübeck and the other Low German-speaking coastal towns along the Baltic were known) were in Boston by the early to mid-thirteenth century when, John Leland suggests, they helped to found the Franciscan Friary (Greyfriars). The earliest reference to it is 1268. The order was founded by St. Francis of Assisi in 1209.[32] During this period, LowGerman speaking merchants were becoming established and had close links with the Greyfriars.

By the early fourteenth century, Boston began to face problems as a result of the decline of its fair and the loss of the wool trade. The cloth export trade, which gradually came to supplant it, fell into the hands of denizens in other towns. But in Boston the Hansards became the dominant group of 'alien' merchants in the town and Boston emerged as the centre for the Hanse/Bergen stockfish trade after 1303. The Hanse were also able to step in as exporters of English cloth out of Boston. As a result, the Hanse remained, in this third period, important and active 'alien' participants in the town's trade when others had left until the Anglo-Hanseatic hostilities from 1468-1474 finally brought everything to a halt.

The early period (c. 1150-1250)

The Hanse were by no means the first foreign merchants to arrive either in the Lincolnshire region or in Boston. Some of Boston's earliest overseas traders were the Scandinavians as well as the 'Gotlanders', although Low German-speaking merchants had arrived on the island by the mid-twelfth century.[33] Other 'alien' merchants arrived in Boston from France – Bordeaux, Toulouse in Gascony; from Flanders (Douai and Ypres) and from Brabant; from Italy (Florence, Lucca) as well as from Norway.[34]

32 Leland's wording is '...Marchauntes of the Stiliard cumming by all partes by est were wont greatly to haunt Boston: and the grey frères toke them yn a manner for the founders of their house, and many Esterlinges were buried thee'. Quoted in Badham (2012) pp.2–3 in Badham and Cockerham. See also Rigby (2012) p. 9 footnote 18 in Badham and Cockerham.

33 Carus-Wilson (1962-63) p. 191-192. Hammel-Kiesow (2015) p. 43 says by 1229 Gotlanders were part of an 'association of merchants from the Roman Empire' with their own seal. Henry III's charter (1237) granted Gotlanders freedom from all tolls and custom on their imports and exports. In other words 'Gotlanders' in England from the early thirteenth century were German merchants.

34 Harden (1978) Fig. 5 p. 10 and Rigby (2012).

Cologne merchants had begun to import large quantities of wine to England by the middle of the twelfth century and were soon granted 'perpetual protection' by Henry II (1154-1189). Cologne men were allowed to sell wine on the same terms as freemen and be treated as the 'King's own men'. They also set up their own guild (*gilda mercatoria teutonicorum*) in London which later became the London Steelyard and together with Bruges, one of the two most important overseas Hanse '*kontore*'. Rigby[35] summarises:

> German merchants were ... present in Boston [in the twelfth century]. At this date, merchants from Cologne virtually monopolised Anglo-German trade, exporting English wool and importing wine, cloth, metalwork and other goods. Cologne merchants were active in Lincolnshire in the twelfth century and can be seen trading at Boston fair in the early thirteenth century. In 1213, for instance, Arnulf Ungfother, merchant of Cologne, was licensed to attend Boston fair to trade along with his cog (*goga sua*) and in 1224 Terricus de Stamford, a Cologne man who dealt in wool, cloth and wine, was exporting goods from Boston.....The purchase of 'greywork', i.e. winter squirrel skins, for the king's use at Boston fair in 1222 may be an early sign of the arrival of the Esterlings in the trade of the port whilst in 1226 the men of Gotland were also claiming exemption from lastage on their trade in Boston.

The middle period (1250-1350)

By the end of the thirteenth century, the provincial east coast towns that figured most prominently in Hanse trade were Boston, Lynn, Hull and Ravenser (now lost to the sea). According to Lappenberg there were 16 Lübeck merchants who were in Boston by 1277, preceded (1272) by merchants from Dortmund who had also settled in the town.[36] Men from Stralsund, Rostock, Deventer, Staveren and Attendorn are all mentioned in documents about the Hanse in Boston in 1303.[37]

35 Rigby (2017).

36 Lappenberg (1851) and Tennenhaus, (1976) pp. 189-193.

37 Lloyd (1991) p. 36 referring to Hansische Urkundenbuch No. 40 and Rigby (2012) p. 11, note 44 say 'it was [always] the 'Esterlings' from towns such as Lübeck, Hamburg,

Although John Leland was writing during the 1530s, long after the height of the wool trade and the fairs in the earlier period, and long after the arrival of the Esterlings in this middle period, his account still remains an invaluable description. His mention of the Hanse in their association with the Greyfriars also points to the Esterlings' significance in the community.[38]

> Mr. Paynel, a gentleman of Boston, told me that since the great and famous fair of old Boston was burnt [in 1288] the town has scarcely ever since reached the same old glory and riches that it once had and was then many, many times richer than it is now. The staple and Steelyard house are still here, but the Steelyard is very little – almost never - occupied. There were, then, four colleges of Friars, altogether, and Merchants of the Steelyard [the Hansards] came to the east coast and spent a great deal of time in Boston. The Grey Friars took them to be founders of their house and many 'Easterlings' [merchants who concentrated their attention on the east coast of England, many of whom in Boston came from Lübeck] were buried there. ... The Easterlings too kept a great house and warehouse for merchandise in Boston [the Steelyard] until Humfrey Litlebyri, merchant of Boston, killed one of the Easterlings during the reign of Edward IV [1461-1483] so that at last the Easterlings left their warehouses in Boston, and since that time the town is sorely decayed. One Mawde Tylney laid the first stone of the good steeple of the parish church of Boston and lies buried underneath. The Tylneys were taken for the founders of three of the four houses of friars in Boston.

The Hanse merchants association with the Greyfriars in Boston was not unusual. Murray discusses the Hanse in Bruges, one of their most important *kontore*, and their close interaction with the Carmelites where they kept archives and a set of master weights and had organised

---

Rostok, Wismar, Stralsund and Danzig who were [most] prominent in Boston'.

38 Leland's original language in Badham (2012) pp. 1-2, Badham and Cockerham from Toulmin–Smith (1964 edition).

burial space in the monastic church, as the Hanse merchants did with the Greyfriars in Boston.[39]

> [The Hanse were]..the first to display a marked preference
> for the mendicant orders and that Bruges was a site of *'studia*
> *generalia'* for the Franciscans, Carmelites and Augustinians ...
> a monastic cosmopolitanism which may have more easily
> attracted foreign merchants. In Bruges the Hanse used the
> Carmelite refectory for meetings [and] tradition even attributed
> to the Hanse a hand in the foundation of the order in Bruges.[40]

In England there had been a close association between the universities and the 'mendicant' orders. Robert Grosseteste, first at Oxford and later as Bishop of Lincoln, was sympathetic and before 1300 each of the five main centres of urban population in Lincolnshire (Lincoln, Stamford, Boston, Grantham and Grimsby) had at least one friary. That Boston had four was, however, exceptional and attests to the importance of the town at that time.

> The foundation of the Boston Franciscan Friary, with its many
> German friars by the easterling community of that town is
> a particularly good example of the importance of the friars
> in these towns. That is, the Franciscan house at Boston was
> founded by German merchants already living there ... No
> more was needed for a friary than a small piece of land, a
> simple building, congregations to hear sermons and charitable
> Christians to give small regular doles.[41]

Nor was the Boston Greyfriars simply a religious centre. 11 tuns of wine stored there was stolen in 1268, suggesting secular arrangements supplemented religion and alms. This was particularly the case if there were both German-speaking friars and German merchants in town and

---

39 A number were buried in the Greyfriars graveyard in Boston, see Owen (1971) and one tombstone, Wissel de Smalenburg (d. 1340), has survived and is now in St. Botolph's church.

40 Murray (2005) p. 225.

41 Owen (1971) p. 52 and p. 85. The earliest reference to the Greyfriars (Franciscans) in Boston is this 1268 date. The Dominicans (Blackfriars) were in Boston by the time of the fire in 1288 which burnt down their friary. The Carmelites were there by 1293, the only one to be established on the west side of the river and the Austins (Augustinians) were there by 1317, close to the Hanseatic Steelyard. Badham (2012) note 18. p. 9.

the Hanse were used to making mutually convenient arrangements such as those with the Carmelites in Bruges.

The late period (c. 1350-1468)

In Boston, as elsewhere, the types of commodities traded shifted and changed over time which meant that the geographical origins of the merchants also changed. The close links at the beginning of the thirteenth century between Boston, Bruges and the north German Baltic towns was superseded by a more tightly orchestrated arrangement, as the Boston, Lübeck and Bergen trade was developed and as the Hanse gained more control over the stockfish trade in Norway. Stockfish was dried (as opposed to salted) and was the cheapest and most popular dish on the fast days of the Catholic church.[42] The Hanse Bergen *kontor* was established there by 1360.

Whilst it is much harder to trace Hanse trade in Boston during the earlier period (1100-1250) it becomes easier once wool and cloth were systematically taxed by the Crown (the source of information presented in tables (b) and (c) above). 'Aliens' also paid custom on cloth from 1303 onwards (denizens from 1347). This coincides with the Hansards most active period in Boston. The administrative organisation set up for customs collections meant that careful record-keeping became a necessity. Revenue collectors and controllers were appointed to lucrative posts granted by the king.[43] As the customs system developed so too did the systematic channelling of wool exports to the so-called 'staple' towns. The Exchequer's enrolled customs accounts have survived[44] and provide a comprehensive source of information about the volumes of England's export trade in wool and cloth in all the staple towns including Boston.

42 Nedkvitne (2014) p. 15.

43 These customs duties began in 1275 (known as the Ancient Custom) for exports of wool, wool-fells and hides for all merchants at 6s 8d. per sack. In 1303 a New Custom was introduced at 3s 4d. per sack of wool for alien merchants only — a total of 10s. for aliens and 6s 8d for denizens. In 1303 the first customs duty on cloth was introduced to be paid by alien merchants only and extended in 1347 to all merchants. Carus-Wilson and Coleman (1963) Appendix III pp.194-195.

44 These are a summary of the 'particulars' about the customs collections in individual towns. The particulars of ports have often survived less well and for Boston they do not survive for almost every year as the enrolled accounts do. Rigby (2005) makes the most of one set for a 20 year period at the end of the fourteenth century. For a detailed account of trade in Boston in this period. Rigby (1983) ch. 4.

Lübeck men in the Bergen *kontor* made use of the Norwegian staple in fish and fish oil. Fish were caught in the far north, cured — turning them into dried stockfish — and then brought to the Bergen staple. By the end of the fourteenth century the Hanse began to displace both the English and the Norwegians handling this trade. But as a result, the Lübeckers then displaced the *Englandfahrer* from Stralsund who complained bitterly of their 'oppression at the hands of Lübeckers' who in turn became *Englandfahrer*.[45] Hans Schulten and Hinrik van den Bure, for example, were citizens of Lübeck and '....authorized signatories and agents of the *Englandfahrer* of Bergen in Norway, *who visit Boston.*'[46]

In England, the Hansards were able to take advantage of the fact that Italians (who had always played a central role in England's cloth exports) moved away from Boston and other east coast ports to the south — Southampton especially. In the ensuing competition between denizen merchants and the Hansards to gain control of what remained of cloth exports on the east coast, the denizens 'gained more control in Lynn and Yarmouth'[47] while the Hansards concentrated on Boston. The result was to consolidate the Bergen 'trade triangle'. By the end of the fourteenth century, Boston was by far the biggest port handling Hanseatic cloth exports.

Hanse merchants from certain towns increasingly concentrated on particular English towns: merchants from Cologne on London; Prussians on Lynn and Hull; Hamburg on Yarmouth and in Boston, mainly merchants from Lübeck who by the late fourteenth century 'made up more than 50% of all Hansards in Boston and ran the steelyard where Hanseatic merchants concentrated their trade and *stayed together during their visits to the town.*'[48] [my italics].

English cloth remained the main Hanse export from Boston from the start of this later period and the Baltic was the final destination for most of it. After the Hanseatic evacuation of Bergen between 1427-1433, their export of English cloth declined.[49]

---

45 Lloyd (1991) p. 41.
46 Burkhardt (2007) p. 68.
47 Burkhardt (2007) pp. 65-85 in Brand, Holm and Müller.
48 Burkhardt (2007) p. 67. Note 19 also references Jenks (1992) p. 464.
49 Nedkvitne (2014).

... when the Hanseatic large-scale engagement in Boston came to an end in the 1460s, denizen merchants [having turned their attention elsewhere] were unable to fill the gap the Hansards' withdrawal left in the market and the total amount of exported cloth from Boston sank dramatically.[50]

Finally, the one political event that cannot be ignored was the impact of Anglo-Hanseatic hostilities which spilled over in 1468 when Denmark seized seven English ships from King's Lynn, breaching agreements, and sailed to Iceland. The English suspected Hanseatic involvement (that the Hanse had helped the Danes to take the Lynn ships) and took action against the Hanse — an easier target — rather than against Denmark directly. From 1468 until 1474 all trade managed by the Hanse in Boston and elsewhere ceased for those years and their properties in England were seized by the English Crown. A separate deal was made with Cologne merchants in London who remained in the London Steelyard although all the Hansards had protested their innocence.[51]

This Anglo-Hanseatic conflict turned out to mark the end as far as the Hanse in Boston was concerned — even though Boston's steelyard, as well as the promise of property in Lynn, were claimed as part of the peace settlement in 1474 (the Treaty of Utrecht). After the Treaty, there was a modest trade in cloth exports in Boston between 1474 until 1485 and a more sporadic trade during the years to the end of the century but 'the Hanseatics were [effectively] finished with Boston.'[52] These factors together helped to concentrate the cloth export trade in London[53] and Boston's role as a major port for overseas trade was lost.

50 Burkhardt (2007) p. 67.

51 Iceland belonged to Denmark and ships from Lynn had sailed to Iceland contravening the agreement with Denmark not to trade in Iceland. That they killed the Danish governor there did not help. Salter (1931) pp. 93-94.

52 Lloyd (1992) p. 277. The Boston Steelyard was included as part of the 1474 settlement. The Bergenfahrer in Lübeck were to supervise the property and there followed several years' correspondence about repairs to it and to the wharves. By this time, the Hanse buildings had been unoccupied for several years having been seized by the English Crown in 1468. In 1481 both the buildings and the wharf were again in such a state of disrepair that the Hansetag granted the Bergenfahrer at Boston £20 to cover necessary work. In 1505, the London kontor once more paid for repairs in Boston and requested Lübeck to encourage the Bergenfahrer to return. But things were never really the same after 1475. See Richards (2007).

53 As happened to England's overseas trade in general during this period, Rigby communication, July 2016.

Hanse residents in Boston

Lloyd claims that 'relations between established members of the *kontor* and the townsfolk of Boston were probably amicable' and we also know that at least one Hanse merchant - as well as merchants from other parts of England - was given membership of one of Boston's most prestigious and wealthy guilds, Corpus Christi. Moreover, Hermann Steynford, another German in the town 'married an English lady and got children in Boston' and was naturalized by the king in 1390.[54] Also, 'numerous foreign 'shipmen' are known to have made Boston or Lynn their home.'[55] But as John Leland recounts, an English merchant is supposed to have killed one of the Esterlings which he claims played a part in their decision to finally abandon the Boston Hanse Steelyard. Relations between England and the Hanse in a precursor to the Anglo-Hanse war also worsened 'when Robert Winnington of Dartmouth captured over 100 ships of the Hanseatic salt fleet in 1449, sparking an international incident.'[56] Moreover, tensions with 'alien' merchants increased throughout the fifteenth century as English merchants became much more vociferous about reciprocal privileges when they travelled overseas to towns such as Danzig.[57]

Hans Brinck was one of the last known *Bergenfahrer* in Boston and died in 1487 having been in partnership with another *Bergenfahrer*. Both came from Lübeck and Nedkvitne[58] says Brinck does not seem to have owned a house in Boston and that he may have rented rooms at the Hanseatic Steelyard there.

The only substantial artefact to remain in the town which definitively points to the importance of the Hanse presence in Boston[59] (from the middle period) is a most beautifully incised Tournai marble slab stone. It was removed from the Greyfriars (Franciscan) graveyard site in 1813 to be brought to St Botolph's parish church, where it now lies in some splendour. It shows a youthful-looking face with curly hair in a long gown and the inscription reads: 'Here lies Wissel called Smalenburg,

54 Fenning (1993) in W.M. Ormrod.
55 Kowaleski (2000) p. 493 in Palliser.
56 Kowaleski (2000) p. 492 in Palliser.
57 Fudge (1995).
58 Nedkvitne (2014) p. 152.
59 Boston's Hanse Steelyard, unlike the Hanse house in King's Lynn, has disappeared.

citizen and merchant of Münster, who died the sixth day after the feast of the birth of the Blessed Virgin Mary AD 1340'. May his soul rest in peace. Amen.[60] He looks very similar to the figures on the brasses of Adam de Walsokne (d. 1349) and Robert Braunch (d. 1364) in St. Margaret's church in King's Lynn. His is certainly a more glamorous image than the 16 rather stern-looking Hanse merchants of the London Steelyard painted by Holbein two hundred years later – an iconographic treasure-trove, but too late to capture the likenesses of the Lübeck merchants and other 'Easterlings' who had earlier frequented the Boston Steelyard.[61]

These Hanseatic burials in Boston and Lynn are important because they also suggest a long-standing amicable association with the towns where these merchants died – an association significant enough for expensive tombstones from west Flanders to be brought to the towns. In the case of Wissel de Smalenburg, we have a German-speaking merchant who wished to remain in Boston rather than to be returned to his own native town of Münster. Unfortunately, very little is known about the man himself.[62] But the manufacture of these tombstones was itself a lucrative, highly-skilled industry, the results of which appear in many towns associated by their trading activities and which point directly to the sophistication of both. Münster was not far away from the wealthy city of Bruges and the Hanse *kontor* there. Nor do we know anything about the owner of Boston's only other likely Hanseatic artefact - a fourteenth century seal belonging to Heinrich Knieval, most probably a merchant living in, or at least visiting, Boston. It was found in South End in 2002.

A Bit of a Mystery: Where was the Hanse Steelyard In Boston?

'Steelyard' is a term which came to be synonymous both with a location for the German merchants in England and with a balance used to weigh items being traded (when spelled with a small 's'). The German word 'stâlhof' is the origin of the term and meant a place where

---

60 Cockerham (2012) pp. 74-99. Unfortunately, very little is known about the man himself, see note 33 p. 79.

61 Holman (1980) pp. 139-158.

62 Cockerham (2012) p. 79.

goods were offered for sale[63] — from 'stâl', a middle, or Low German word which meant 'a merchants sample' or 'pattern' and ' hof' which meant yard or courtyard.[64] In short, a 'steelyard' has nothing to do with 'steel'.[65] What it came to mean was the buildings used by the Hanse merchants when they came to England, above all in London. But the Hanse also set up smaller 'Steelyards' or 'outposts' in port towns such as Boston and Lynn. All the Hanse buildings in England, except in King's Lynn, have been destroyed and significant archaeological work would now need to be conducted to be more sure of the original sites were we to try and locate them.

Nevertheless, we do have an original description of the buildings comprising Boston's Hanse Steelyard:

> an old house or complex with ten rooms and seven chimneys and associated rear buildings in which there were 11 booths ... [and that it was] ... dilapidated and needed repair to secure it against the winter of 1475/76.[66]

The Historic Environment Record's description of the likely site for the Hanse Steelyard land and buildings appears in the Lincolnshire Historical Environment Record, document MLI 12703.[67]

> A steelyard or Customs House [note discussion below] is first mentioned in 1585 and formerly stood near the present site of St. John's Terrace. An acre of land 'at the Steelyards' is mentioned in 1601. In 1660 the reversion of a messuage called 'The Steelyards' and four acres of hempland called 'Steelyards

---

63 Dollinger (1964) p.102.

64 Jansen (2008) p. 66.

65 Norman (1902) p. 2 says firmly that 'after careful study of the evidence at present available, I have come to the conclusion that the word has nothing to do with steel [stahl — including an "h" does indeed mean steel in German] or with a weighing machine, but that it is an anglicised form (one can hardly call it a mistranslation) of the German "Stahlhof" in early times spelled "Stalhof" — a name applied in the year 1320 to ground east of Windgoose Lane."

66 'Das Kontor zu Boston wurde durch sie am 23 Juni 1475 in Besitz genommen ... [es war] zum Zeitpunkt der Übernahme eyn alt huys mit zehn Kammern und einem dazugehörigen Hinterhaus in dem sich elf Budun befanden' in Jorn (2000) p. 408. But the original description is found in Hansische Urkundenbuch, 10 No. 477.

67 Lincolnshire County Archive, Environmental Heritage Record, accessed April, 2016 for documents MLI12703 1540-1599 and ML83372, 1401-1650.

Green' was purchased by the Corporation from Mr. Earl for £260. In 1663 The Steelyards and cellars, orchard, garden and land were rented for £20. In 1674, two jetties were put down at The Steelyards and in 1693 the materials of The Steelyards buildings were sold to Francis Ayscough for £120. This building is mentioned by Leland as standing in his time, but it was little occupied.

The area shaded on the map on the next page lies on the river bank in what is now South Terrace. If the location of the Hanse Steelyard in this area is correct, as shown on Hill's map on page 49, then it stood just outside the medieval boundary formed by the Barditch, some distance from the centre of medieval Boston.

Current confusions

In 1994 there was an archaeological excavation of the St John's Terrace site and the subsequent Baseline Report (1995)[68] included maps showing medieval sites in Boston. On these, there are question marks at two possible sites for Boston's Hanse Steelyard: the first in the Mart Yard (now the location of Boston Grammar School) close to where the Franciscan Friary (Greyfriars) once stood. Secondly one for the site shown at South Terrace the same as Pishey Thompson's 'Steelyards Green' area. This is the accompanying description in the Report.

A further development of paramount importance to the town was the arrival of Hanseatic merchants from the Baltic, soon after 1259 (Thompson, p. 366). They established a Steelyard (Customs House) towards the south of the town, possibly in the region of the Grammar School, adjacent to the Mart Yard, the place where stalls were set up at the fairs and markets. However, post-medieval references suggest that the Steelyard may have been located in the vicinity of South Terrace, an area later called 'Steelyard Green' (Thompson, p. 247). Excavations at the former General Hospital site did find evidence for high-status buildings, although the ground plan retrieved was insufficient to identify the presence of a Steelyard or the Austin friary [nearby].

68 Cope-Faulkner, Hambly and Young (1995).

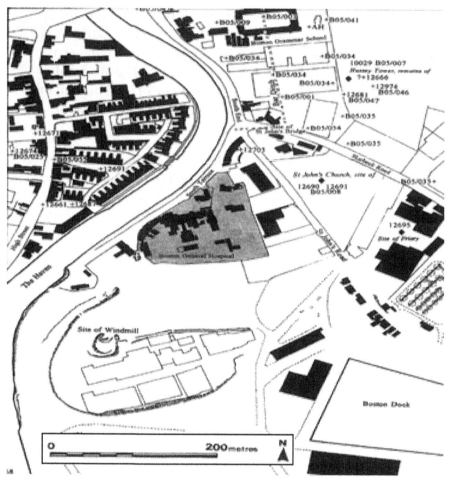

Steelyards Green, Archaeological Project Services Report (1994).

There are four problems with this paragraph:

1. The suggestion that the Hanse Steelyard could have been in the Mart Yard rather than in the South Terrace site.

    But the problem here is that —

2. The Mart Yard only dates from the late sixteenth century and we know that the Hanse Steelyard was in Boston considerably earlier than this.[69]

3. The suggestion that the (old) Customs House is the same building as the Hanse Steelyard.

---

69 There is only evidence of the Mart Yard being used for trade in the late sixteenth century, Rigby, communication July 2016; see also Rigby (2017).

4. The possibility that Thompson himself may have confused the two meanings of the Hanse Steelyard, in the sense of place, with the term 'steelyard', in the sense of a 'weigh beam', conflating what are likely to have been two different buildings in two different locations – the old Customs House and the buildings that made up Boston's Hanseatic Steelyard.[70]

The speculations in the Report suggests that the South Terrace location is the favoured site for the Hanseatic Steelyard buildings (see Figure 1). And if point 2. is correct, then the Steelyard location could not in any case have been at the Mart Yard. During the excavations, they found that:

Adjacent [to the remains of a brick structure] was a stone structure which may have been a warehouse, and which may be associated with the Hanseatic League – a powerful group of German merchants who established a headquarters building (*kontor*) in Boston as early as 1260. **Therefore it is possible that well preserved remains of this building exist beneath South Terrace to the west and beneath and beyond the modern road** ...[my emphasis][71]

---

70 Thompson (1856)

Extract 1: 'In the Utrecht treaty of 1474 the place was called Staelhof or Stylyard, which is explained to signify the spot where the great public beam and balance stood, by which all goods were weighed on landing in order to ascertain and secure the King's toll.' (p. 326)

Extract 2: 'The foreign merchants trading with Boston [and elsewhere] were those known by the title of Merchants of the Steelyard. This body of traders is said to have existed in the time of the Anglo Saxons: they were originally Germans residing in London; and it is recorded of them that they then paid annually to the king for his protection two pieces of grey cloth, and one piece of brown cloth, ten pounds of pepper, five pairs of gloves and two casks of wine. They derived their title as Merchants of the Steelyard from the circumstance of their trading almost entirely by weight, and using the steelyard [beam] as their weighing apparatus.'

Extract 3: 'The ancient customs-house at Boston was called the 'Stylyard's House', probably from the weighing of goods there by means of a steelyard in order to ascertain the duties payable on them. Many merchants from Calais, Cologne, Ostend and other places resided in Boston from the time of Edward I [1282–1307)] but it was not until the removal of the Staple to Boston [in 1369] that any company or association of merchants was formed there. Camden calls the merchants who settled here after the establishment of the Staple the merchants of the Hanseatic League and says they founded their guild or house here.' (p. 329)

71 Cope-Faulkner, Hambly and Young (1995).

Taking everything together it seems almost certain that Boston's Hanse Steelyard was in South Terrace. The map of medieval Boston in Francis Hill's (1948) *Medieval History of Lincoln* is the only reconstruction of the medieval layout of the town which includes a site for Boston's Hanseatic Steelyard in South Terrace (once St. John's Terrace). We also know that whatever the course of the river then,[72] the Hanse Steelyard must have been on the riverbank since repairs to the 'staithes' (or quayside) are mentioned in correspondence about maintaining the property following the Treaty of Utrecht in 1474.

But it still remains unclear what exactly the connection was (if any) between the Hanse Steelyard and the old Customs House. Another Historic Environment Record report, MLI83372, refers to excavations at a different site in South End (Haven House) which 'may possibly have been the old Customs House known to have been in the area' contradicting their statement in MLI12703 above. But if the speculation in MLI183372 is correct and this was the site of the old Customs House in South End — then the old Customs House was indeed a different building from the Hanse Steelyard. It also makes sense for the old Customs House to have been here, not far from the site of the new Customs House, built in 1725 and still situated a little further along South End today.

Given that neither the buildings in Boston nor those of the London Steelyard survive, King's Lynn's Hanse House is now unique in England as the only Hanse building left above ground. It is tempting to suppose that Boston's was similar in structure. After all, the function and purposes of all the Hanse *kontore* were similar[73] - personal safety for foreign ('alien') merchants and secure storage for their goods. In King's Lynn it is a four-sided rectangular building with a courtyard through the centre allowing warehousing on the ground floor and rooms above. In Lynn, traders from Lübeck, Hamburg, Bremen and Danzig had earlier rented or bought houses in the town — as frequently happened elsewhere - Bruges is one of the best examples of this and this clearly happened in Boston too.[74]

---

72 I am grateful to Neil Wright for raising this when we first discussed a possible Hanse Steelyard location in Boston.

73 Lappenburg's map of the London Steelyard — a grand complex — is reproduced in Norman (1909). Its remains now lie under Cannongate station.

74 For a drawing of the King's Lynn Hanse house see Parker (1971) p. 117.

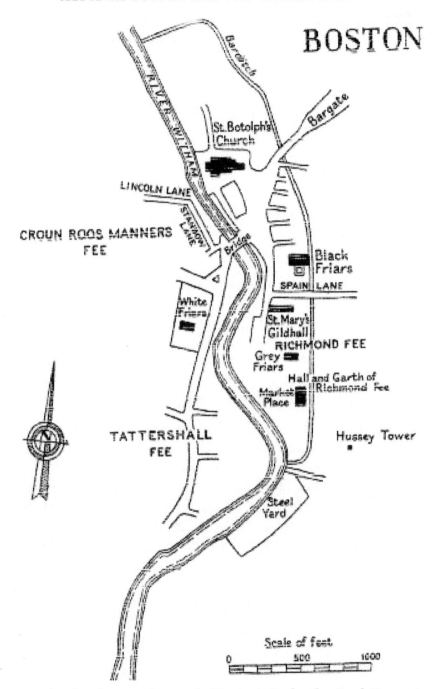

A map of medieval Boston showing the Hanseatic Steelyard at South Terrace, in F. Hill (1948) 'Medieval Lincoln', Archaeological Project Services Report (1994).

Writing about the rich possibilities for further archaeological work on medieval Boston Gillian Harden suggested nearly 40 years ago that:

> The excavation of a riverside site should be undertaken. The site should be one where reclamation from the river has occurred, preserving the quays which lined the Witham in the medieval period. The associated warehouse or house should be excavated with the quay, [which would give] a fairly comprehensive picture of a unit that was vital to the economy of Boston. [75]

Given the discussion above, Harden's call-to-arms seems that much more pertinent and more recently Ayers, also a medieval archaeologist writes:

> Most of the Hanseatic residences seem to have been gated communities enabling control by the Hanse of contact between their merchants and the indigenous population as well as protective storage for goods. Surviving physical evidence is scarce across northern Europe, although documentary evidence can help towards an understanding of their organisation (such evidence is particularly good for Novgorod). [76]

Should therefore both medieval archaeologists and historians look more closely at the Hanse Steelyard in Boston, once such an important part of Boston's town and maritime community? It might even offer a focus to investigate smaller Hanseatic kontore sites more generally. In doing so, we might learn a great deal more about the Hanse merchants and others who lived and worked with them, an example and a reminder of the importance of economic interconnection both now and long ago.

Bibliography

Archaeological Project Services Report (1994) *Evaluation Excavation at the General Hospital Site, Boston Lincolnshire*, July pp. 1-15 plus appendices.

75 Harden (1978) p. 36.

76 Ayers (2016) p. 126. His book does something rare which is to help us to understand an entire geographic region in a different way: that the North Sea (until quite recently The German Ocean) can be seen and better understood historically as one big lake creating similar communities along the shores north, east and west and stretching right up through the Baltic to Russia. We need such perspectives now more than ever.

Arnold-Baker, C. (1996) 'Hanse Towns History', in *Companion to British History*, Longcross

Ayers, B. (2013) ch. 3 'Cities, Cogs and Commerce: Archaeological Approaches to the Medieval Culture of the North Sea World' pp.d 63-81 in D. Bates and Liddiard, R. (eds) *East Anglia and its North Sea World in the Middle Ages*, Woodbridge

---------(2016) *The German Ocean. Medieval Europe around the North Sea*, Equinox, Sheffield

Badham, S. (2012) ch. 1 'Introduction' pp 1-5 in Badham, S. and P. Cockerham (eds) *'The beste and fayrest of al Lincolnshire'. The Church of St. Botolph, Boston, Lincolnshire, and its Medieval Monuments*, BAR British Series 554

Burkhardt, M. (2007) 'One hundred years of thriving commerce at a major English sea port. The Hanseatic Trade at Boston between 1370 and 1470' pp. 65-85 in Brand, H., Holm, P. and L. Müller (eds) *The dynamics of economic culture in the North Sea and Baltic Region (c. 1250-1700)*, vol. 1, Hilversum

----------- (2015) ch. 4 'Kontors and Outposts' pp. 127-161 in Donald J. Harreld (ed) *A Companion to the Hanseatic League*, Brill, Leiden

Carus-Wilson, E.M. (1962-63) 'The medieval trade of the ports of the Wash, *Medieval Archaeology* 6-7 pp. 182-201

----------- (1954) *Medieval Merchant Venturers*, Methuen & Co

Carus-Wilson, E.M. and O. Coleman (1963) *England's Export Trade*, Clarendon Press, Oxford

Childs, W. (1990) *The Trade and Shipping of Hull 1300-1500*, East Yorkshire Local History Society

---------- (2013) ch. 9 'East Anglia's Trade in the North Sea World', pp. 188-203 in D. Bates and Liddiard, R. (eds) *East Anglia and its North Sea World in the Middle Ages*, Woodbridge

Cockerham, P. (2012) ch. 5 'Incised slab commissions in fourteenth century Boston' pp. 74-99 in S. Badham and P. Cockerham (eds) *'The best and fairest of al Lincolnshire'. The church of St. Botolphs, Boston Lincolnshire and its Medieval Monuments*, BAR British Series 554

Cope-Faulkner, P. J. Hambly and J. Young (1995) *Boston Town Historic Environment Baseline Study*, Heritage Trust of Lincolnshire, Heckington

Dollinger, P. (1963) *The German Hansa*, MacMillan

Dover, P. (1970) *The Early Medieval History of Boston AD 1086-1400*, The History of Boston Project No. 2, Richard Kay Publications

Ewert, U.C and S Selzer (2015) ch. 5 'Social Networks' p. 162-193 in Donald J. Harreld (ed) *A Companion to the Hanseatic League*, Brill

Fenning, H. (1993) 'The Guild of corpus Christi, in the Guilds in Boston', pp. 35-44 in W.M. Ormrod (ed), *The Guilds in Boston*, Pilgrim College, University of Nottingham

Fudge, J. (1995) *Cargoes, Embargoes and Emissaries*, Toronto University Press

Gurnham, R. (2014) *The Story of Boston*, The History Press

Hammel-Kiesow, R. (2015) ch. 1 'The Early Hanses' pp. 15-63 in Harreld, Donald J. (ed) *The Companion to The Hanseatic League*, Brill

Harden, G. (1978) *Medieval Boston and its Archaeological Implications*, South Lincolnshire Archaeological Unit, Heckington

Haward, W.I. (1933) The Trade of Boston in the Fifteenth Century *Lincolnshire Architecture and Archaeology Society*, XLI, pp. 169-178

Hill, J.W.F. (1948) *Medieval Lincoln*, Cambridge University Press

Jahnke, C. (2015) ch. 6 'The Baltic Trade' pp. 194-240 in Donald J. Harreld (ed) *The Companion to the Hanseatic League*, Brill

Jansen, V. (2008) 'Trading Places: counting Houses and the Hanseatic 'Steelyard' in *King's Lynn in King's Lynn and the Fens. Medieval Art, Architecture and Archaeology*, John McNeill (ed), The British Archaeological Association conference Transactions XXXI

Jenks, S. (1992) *England, die Hanse und Preussen. Handel und Diplomatie 1377-1474*, Quellen und Darstellungenen zur hansischen Geschichte NF 38, 3 volumes

Jorn, N. (2000) *'With money and blood'. Der Londoner Stalhof im spanungsfeld der englische-hansischen Beziehungen im 15 und 16 Jahrhundert*

Kowaleski, M. (2000) 'Port towns: England and Wales 1300-1540,' pp. 467-94 in D. Palliser (ed) The *Cambridge Urban History of Britain*, Vol. 1 600-1540

Lappenberg, J.M. (1851) *Urkundliche Geschichte des Hansischen Stahlhofes zu London*

Leland, J. in L. Toulmin Smith (1964 edition) *The itinerary of John Leland in or about the years 1535-1543*, five volumes

Ludat, H. (1951) 'Ein Zeugnis westfälisch-englischer Beziehungen im Mittelalter – die grahplatte eines hansischen Kaufmans aus Münster in England', Westfalen – *Hefte für Geschichte Kunst und Volkskunde 29*

Lloyd, T.H. (1977) *The English Wool Trade in the Middle Ages*, Cambridge University Press

---------- (1991) *England and the German Hanse 1157-1611. A study of their trade and commercial diplomacy*, Cambridge University Press

---------- (1982) *Alien Merchants in England in the High Middle Ages*, The Harvester Press

Miller, E. and J. Hatcher (1995) *Medieval England: Towns, Commerce and Crafts 1086-1348*, Longman

Moore E. Wedemeyer (1985) *The Fairs of Medieval England*, Pontifical Institute of Mediaeval Studies

Murray, J. M. (2005) *Bruges, Cradle of Capitalism, 1280-1390*, Cambridge University Press

Nedkvitne, A. (2014) *The German Hanse and Bergen 1100-1600*, Böhlau Verlag, Köln: Quellen und Darstellungen zur Hansischen Geschichte, Neue Folge Band LXX.

Norman, P. (1909) *Notes on the Later History of the Steelyard in London*, J.B. Nichols and Sons

Owen, D. (1984) The Beginnings of the Port of Boston' in *A Prospect of Lincolnshire in honour of Ethel H. Rudkin*, N. Field and A. White (eds), County Offices, Lincoln

Owen, D. (1971) *Church and Society in Medieval Lincolnshire*, Lincolnshire Local History Society Vol. 5

Parker, V. (1971) *The Making of King's Lynn*, Phillimore & Co.

Postan, M.M. (1933) III 'The Economic and Political Relations of England and the Hanse from 1400 to 1475' pp. 91-153 in Power, E. and M.M. Postan (eds) *Studies in English Trade in the Fifteenth Century*, Routledge

Richards, P. (2007) 'The Hanseatic League and Eastern England in the Middle Ages', talk for Gresham College, 14 June

----------2015) *England and the Hanseatic League: Past and Present*, unpublished essay for a lecture at the Hamburg Chamber of Commerce, 29 October 2014

Richards, P. and K. Friedland (eds) (2005) *Essays in Hanseatic History*, Larks Press

Rigby, S.H. (1983) *Boston and Grimsby in the Middle Ages*, unpublished PhD University of London

---------- (1984) 'Boston and Grimsby in the Middle Ages: an administrative contrast', *Journal of Medieval History*, 10, 1 pp. 51-66

---------- (2005) *The Overseas Trade of Boston in the Reign of Richard II*, Lincoln Record Society

---------- (2012) Chapter 2 'Medieval Boston: Economy, Society and Administration' pp. 6-28 in S. Badham and P. Cockerham *'The beste and fairest of al Lincolnshire'. The Church of St. Botolph, Boston, Lincolnshire and its Medieval Monuments'*, BAR British Series 554

---------- (2017) 'Boston c.1086-1225: A Medieval Boom Town' *Occasional Papers in Lincolnshire History and Archaeology*

Salter, F.R. (1931) The Hanse, Cologne and the crisis of 1468', *The Economic History Review*, Vol. 3, No. 1 pp. 93-100.

Summerson, H. (2014) 'Calamity and Commerce: the Burning of Boston Fair in 1288' in C.M. Barron and A.F. Sutton (eds) *The medieval merchant, Harlaxton Medieval Studies*, Vol. XXIV, Shaun Tyas

Swanson, H. (1999) *Medieval British Towns*, Palgrave

Tennenhaus, Dr and Mrs. M (1976) 'Hanseatic Merchants in England. Boston.' *Transactions of Monumental Brass Society* Vol. XI pp. 189-193

Thompson, P. (1856) *The history and antiquities of Boston and the hundred of Skirbeck*,

Veale, E.M. (1966) *The English Fur Trade in the later Middle Ages*, Oxford University Press

Acknowledgements

This essay is based on a presentation to the Hanse and Archaeology Symposium, Marriott's Warehouse, King's Lynn May 16th, 2015. New to the field of *medieval* economic history (my background is Development Studies, primarily in India and in Political Economy at the University of Sydney) I could not have begun without Stephen Rigby's work on medieval Boston and his generous, astonishingly speedy, responses to my work during the last four years. I thank Brian Ayers and Wendy Childs for their lucid teaching and their willingness to comment on written material. I again thank Brian for coming to Boston to discuss the possible site of the Hanse Steelyard – I couldn't have been more fortunate in meeting them all. Neil Wright is an encyclopaedic authority on the history of the town and has also been generous with meetings and comments. Steve Lumb and Jenny Young first alerted me to the archaeological discussion.

Thanks, despite the pain inflicted, to Paul Richards for his persistence in inviting me both to speak and write for the Hanse Symposium. His own extensive work on the Hanse in King's Lynn and his ongoing efforts to bring Boston's Hanseatic history into the limelight alongside King's Lynn and the other east coast port towns was also crucial at all stages. Thanks to all at the re-formed History of Boston Project who initially gave me a platform — particularly Martin and Alison Fairman and encouragement from Mike Peberdy, Lindsey McBarron and Judy Cammack. They and others were all part of Boston's successful application to join the New Hanse in 2015 (building on John and Judy Cammack's earlier efforts) and in forming the Boston Hanse Group in 2016. Thanks to Luke Skerritt at Boston Guildhall. Paul Kenny, Alison Austin and Richard Austin, successive Mayors of Boston Borough Council from 2013-2016, and a number of councillors who during that period acted in support, as did Rachel and Rob Lauberts, of Boston Big Local to make Boston's application a success. I hope we will all see the benefits to the town in the long term. Last but not least to Gavin, my partner of 28 years, who enriches every single day (well mostly) and to my two extraordinary sons, Ewan and Sam.

Ship graffiti in East Anglian churches: a reflection of maritime interventions?[1]

Matthew Champion

In recent centuries the tendency of the British, as an island race, has been to consider themselves as set apart from the rest of Europe. A historical anomaly that floats graciously (or not) off the western coast of the mainland, detached from it politically, economically and socially on all occasions, with only the most unusual and reluctant of military interventions, when an island's defence looks under threat. As a result the traditional British view of their own history has tended to be insular and inward looking.[2] Whilst historical styles and trends may be recognised as being present in both Britain and the continent, it is rare that they are seen as a cogent part of a whole; leading instead to arguments and debates as to which side of the narrow stretch of sea influenced the other. Whilst such a watery barrier did indeed exist, historians and archaeologists are now beginning to truly question just what a real impediment it was.[3] Analysis of everything from Bronze-Age metal working technology, to

1 Sections of this article dealing with ship graffiti characteristics were previously published as Champion, M., 'Medieval Ship Graffiti in English Churches: Meaning and Function', The Mariners Mirror, 101:3, 343–350

2 Paxman, J, *The English: A portrait of a people*, Penguin (1999)

3 Bates, D, & Liddiard, R., *East Anglia and its North Sea world in the Middle Ages*, Boydell (2013)

the stylistic art works and coinage of the Iron Age, most certainly suggest it was no impediment to trade. Indeed, when turning our eyes towards the medieval period it soon becomes clear that the 'silver sea' acted less like a 'moat defensive to a house', and more like a commercial super-highway that allowed and enabled the large scale trade of goods, people and ideas to take place on an unprecedented level.

Perhaps nowhere has this reassessment become more clear in recent decades than in studies focussed upon East Anglia. Britain's most easterly region has been the gateway for European influence, migration, trade and, upon occasion, conquest. Indeed, even today the area shares strong links with its nearby European neighbours, and in most historical periods economic and cultural links between East Anglia and the continent were far stronger than they were with the far west of Britain. In large part this was the result of the coastal and maritime trade that proliferated from the busy east coast ports of places like Great Yarmouth, Lowestoft, Ipswich, Dunwich and, of course, King's Lynn. The trade that flowed from these ports around the 'North Sea basin' during the Middle Ages, particularly by organisations such as the Hansa, brought a wealth to the region that can still be seen in almost every town and village to this day. The most prominent reminder of this wealth that once streamed throughout the region, awash on the back of the continental wool trade, are the many hundreds of quite magnificent and expensive medieval churches that still dominate the area. It would appear that even the lowliest of East Anglian villages, now only a handful of houses scattered across the parish, can still boast a church of near cathedral-like proportions and complexity.

Each East Anglian church is a minor masterpiece of medieval craftsmanship in its own right. Each different, but each telling the story of a parish, a community and, above all, the story of the individuals who worshiped within its walls. Each church stands as a testament to the wealth that trade once brought to the region; with alabaster from Nottinghamshire adoring the altar, cast bronze lecterns from the Low Countries, and carved timbers from as far away as the Baltic. The walls were once bright with expensive pigments, some having travelled across half the world from places such as Afghanistan and Persia, all lit through windows filled with stained glass from the finest workshops in Europe. And it is here, within our individual churches, that we can find first-hand accounts of the lives of the people who lavished such wealth upon a single building — quite literally etched into the walls.

Medieval graffiti has long been overlooked as a major historical resource.[4] However, recent large scale surveys of medieval churches, which began in East Anglia over five years ago, are beginning to change our perceptions of the value we place upon these writings on the wall.[5] To date tens of thousands of previously unrecorded inscriptions have come to light, with representations of just about every medieval activity to be found amongst the graffiti. However, in contrast to many modern graffiti inscriptions, it is clear that the vast majority of medieval examples have a spiritual aspect associated with their creation. Alongside the more formal Latin prayers are many thousands of other inscriptions that appear to directly relate to aspects of faith and belief within medieval society. However, one particular type of graffiti inscription, known as 'ship graffiti', has attracted a great deal of interest from both archaeologists and historians for what it might be able to tell us concerning ships and seafaring during the later Middle Ages.[6] These carved images of ships are to be found in churches across Britain and Europe. However, the scale of the new surveys has resulted in archaeologists being able to identify many hundreds of new examples, meaning that the inscriptions can now be re-examined as a distinct and separate group of material — and the results are highly intriguing.

Previous studies, limited in the number of examples available for study, suggested that ship graffiti was something that was largely found in churches near ports and coastal areas.[7] Whilst there are certainly concentrations of ship graffiti in coastal regions, the more recent surveys have highlighted the fact that examples are not solely confined

4   Until recently only one full length work has appeared upon the subject — Pritchard, V., *English Medieval Graffiti*, Cambridge University Press (1967)

5   The multi-award winning Norfolk Medieval Graffiti Survey (www.medieval-graffiti. co.uk) began in 2010. Since that time almost a dozen other county surveys have been established.

6   See — Brady, K. & Corlett, C., 'Holy Ships: Ships on Plaster at Medieval Ecclesiastical Sites in Ireland', Archaeology Ireland, Vol. 18, No. 2, (Summer 2004) pp. 28 – 31; Emden, A. B., 'Graffiti of medieval ships from the Church of St Margaret at Cliffe, Kent', The Mariners Mirror: Journal of the Society for Nautical Research 8 (1922); Gardiner, M., 'Graffiti and their use in Late Medieval England', Ruralia, Vol. 6, Turnhout Brepols (2007), pp. 265 – 276

7   Pritchard, *English Medieval Graffiti*

to the coast, with many inscriptions being recorded as far inland as the counties of Hertfordshire, Wiltshire and Leicestershire.[8] In purely statistical terms though it must be conceded that nearly 90 per cent of inscriptions are located on the coast or its immediate hinterland. However, if analysed purely in terms of sites containing examples of ship graffiti, rather than the individual examples themselves, then that percentage diminishes to a little above 65 percent; the result of coastal sites often containing large numbers of examples within a single church, as opposed to the inland sites which may contain only one or two examples.

During even the most cursory examination surviving examples of medieval ship graffiti show that many of them have a number of general characteristics in common; characteristics that are often, but not always, shared with manuscript and other contemporary depictions.[9] These characteristics only ever relate to the majority of inscriptions, and there are exceptions to almost all the general conclusions – but the characteristics are present in enough examples to make them noteworthy. In some cases certain characteristics may be shared by as many as 90 per cent of examples, in others cases characteristics may be shared by only a little above half of the recorded examples. It must also be noted that whilst regional differences may account for a number of individual characteristics these have been difficult to identify. As Ian Friel has pointed out,' the answer here, as with the documents, is to avoid an over reliance on any single source, and to look at representational trends'.[10] In general, and rather surprisingly, ship graffiti shows remarkably little variation wherever it is found; suggesting that traditions associated with the creation of these images were universally known and understood throughout the country, and indeed the rest of northern Europe.

These main characteristics of pre-reformation ship graffiti identified to date are:

    1.   Full hull. The ships are invariably shown in full profile, from either left or right, and with the hull visible from the keel line

8   Champion, M., *Medieval Graffiti: the lost voices of England's churches*, Ebury Press (2015)

9   Flatman, J., *Ships and Shipping in Medieval Manuscripts*, British Library Publishing (2009)

10 Friel,I., *The Good ship*, British Museum Press (1995) p.18

upwards and not, as they would most often have been seen in reality, from the waterline upwards.

2. Furled sails. The majority of ship graffiti depicts vessels with either no sails visible or, where more elaborate depictions are to be found, with sails furled.

3. Anchors. A high proportion of ship images are shown with ropes or hawsers leading away from the bow of stern. At the end of these ropes an anchor will often be crudely depicted. The rope lines can upon occasion be rather long, with the anchor shown on another face of a stone pier, or geographically remote from the ship itself. As a result these anchors have often been overlooked.

4. Single mast. Despite the fact that multi-masted vessels are well attested from the late medieval period the majority of ship graffiti are depicted single masted. There are noted exceptions at sites such as Blakeney, Norfolk.

5. Crew. Although a less widely recognised characteristic, a number of vessels are shown with human figures aboard. Whether such figures represent crew members or passengers is indeterminable.

6. Rigging. The majority of ship graffiti, no matter how crude, invariably contains an attempt at depicting rigging lines. In the single masted vessels the vast majority of rigging lines run towards the stern, suggesting a stepped mast.

7. Sea-going vessels. Almost all ship graffiti depicts vessels with a 'mast-head', or 'Crows nest', even those created many dozens of miles inland. Mast heads are not usually found on riverine vessels, suggesting that all the ship graffiti, without obvious exception, depicts sea-going vessels.

Whilst a lot of these observations are just that — wide-ranging generalisations — they also tend to ignore the fact that, to an outside viewer, many of the examples of ship graffiti we come across actually all look pretty much the same. There are certainly massive variations in the quality of inscriptions. Highly detailed and realistic images of ships are rather rare, with examples such as that found at Bassingham in Lincolnshire, which looks as though it has just sailed off the page of a medieval manuscript, being amongst the very finest depictions seen

A very fine example of a late medieval or Tudor ship graffiti from Bassingham in Lincolnshire.

to date.[11] At the other end of the spectrum there are very many depictions that are so crudely done, such as those on the chancel arch at Burnham Norton, that it is questionable in some cases as to whether they were actually meant to represent ships in the first place. However, the majority of examples fall into the middle ground of images that are clearly meant to show sailing vessels, and show many of the main features of a medieval ship, but are no great works of art or technical drawing.

Meaning and Understanding

Given the number of these inscriptions that have been recorded the main questions must be two fold; why are there so many images of ships in churches even many miles inland, and do they have any particular significance? Are they simply the random doodles of bored choirboys, or was their creation linked to a deeper meaning and function?

Firstly, it is worth remembering that ships and ship images were no strangers to the inside of the churches of medieval England. The name of the main public area of the church, the nave, was actually derived directly from the Latin term 'navis', meaning 'ship' or 'vessel', and

11 This example is misidentified by Pritchard as being at Marton.

references dating back to the very earliest days of the Christian church direct that churches should be built 'long ... so it will be like a ship'. As early as the fourth century the role of Bishop is described as being like 'one that is a commander of a great ship', and that of Deacon as 'like the mariners and managers of the ship'.[12] Whilst the church itself might have been likened to a ship it also contained numerous ship images, from those contained in medieval wall paintings (especially the ever popular St Christopher), to those accompanying the images and statues of the saints. In East Anglia the ship as a decorative motif also made appearances on carved woodwork, such as pews or bench-ends, with high quality examples coming from St Nicholas chapel in Kings Lynn (now in the Victoria and Albert museum) and Thornham church on the north Norfolk coast.[13] Lastly, and perhaps most obviously, many English churches actually once had detailed models of ships hanging from the intricately carved timbers of the roof. Often known today as 'church ships', these models were made as votive offerings to the church, offered in thanksgiving for a safe return from a perilous journey, and they were once a common sight in churches up and down the country. Although very few English examples now survive a number are shown in late medieval woodcut illustrations, and several post-medieval examples can still be seen at the church of All Souls by the Tower in London. However, the most obvious manifestation of these votive ships is the over nine hundred examples of small model ships, of various ages, that can be seen today displayed in the churches of Denmark.[14]

The close links between the medieval church and ship imagery mean that it should come as no surprise to find multiple examples amongst the graffiti inscriptions being recorded. However, the sheer number of examples of ship graffiti that have been discovered, and the manner in which they are distributed inside the church, certainly makes them highly noteworthy — and may give us a number of tantalising clues as to the reason for their creation in the first place.

The church at Blakeney on the north Norfolk coast is full of early graffiti inscriptions, including everything from elaborate illuminated medieval

12 Tyack, Rev. G. S., *Lore and Legend of the English Church*, William Andrews and Co (1899) pp.101–2

13 V&A museum number W.16-1921

14 Harley, B., *Church Ships: a handbook of votive and commemorative models*, Canterbury Press (1994) pp.16–18

text inscriptions to simple geometric designs, which have been the subject of an intensive long-term study by historian John Peake.[15] What Peake noted was that, despite early graffiti inscriptions being present all over the structure, the many examples of ship graffiti to be found in the church were all located in one area. Without exception the ship imagery was entirely confined to the pillars of the south arcade, with a massive concentration of over 30 examples located on the easternmost pier. Ranging from the elaborate to the very crude, these images of ships are believed to have been created over a period of one or two centuries. Each image respects the space of those around it, meaning that none of the images significantly overlap each other,

Ship graffiti from St. Nicholas's church, Blakeney, showing a single masted vessel most probably representing a North Sea cog.

leaving the surface of the stonework quite literally covered in small ships. This pier faces the side altar, and a now restored image niche in the south wall, and the majority of the ship inscriptions clearly face towards these features. Peake's research has shown that the side altar in this position was for the churches dedicatory saint — Saint Nicholas, patron saint of those in peril upon the sea — and suggests a link between the imagery and the cult of the saint.

The possible link between the cult of St Nicholas and the ship graffiti is not confined only to Blakeney. The church of St Thomas, Winchelsea, was originally built in the late thirteenth century as the centrepiece of Edward I's planned town that was designed to replace

15 Peake, J., 'Graffiti and Devotion in Three Maritime Churches' in Heslop, T.A., Mellings, E. & Thofner, M., (eds) Art, Faith and Place in East Anglia: from Prehistory to the Present, Boydell Press (2013)

'Old Winchelsea' after a series of catastrophic storms and floods had all but laid it waste.[16] The church was originally constructed on cathedral like proportions, although today little remains but the east end, and there is still some debate as to whether the building was ever fully completed. Here too, as at Blakeney, the church contains a very large number of graffiti inscriptions, scattered across the remaining

fabric. However, all of the examples of ship graffiti are to be found on the two piers located at the eastern end of the north aisle, facing towards the side chapel and side altar — again known to have been dedicated to St Nicholas. At sites such as St Nicholas' chapel in Kings Lynn the relationship is not quite so clear cut. Whilst ship graffiti has been recorded there in the south porch, the interior of the building has been much

Ship graffiti throughout Europe share a number of similar characteristics, with this example of a late medieval cog, from St. Thomas's church, Winchelsea, being all but identical to examples from Norfolk, Suffolk and further afield.

restored, removing any obvious distribution patterns that were once present.[17] However, the presence of ship graffiti at so many sites does strongly suggest a clear link between some, but certainly not all, of the ship graffiti and the cult of St Nicholas.

The distribution patterns found at Blakeney and Winchelsea are also echoed, albeit in an unusual manner, in the tiny north Norfolk church of Burnham Norton. The church is notable today for its superb early font, its lovely surviving medieval rood screen, and the exceptionally

16 Martin, D. and B., *New Winchelsea, Sussex: a medieval port town*, English Heritage/HMP (2004)

17 Champion, M., *Graffiti Survey Record, St Nicholas Chapel, Kings Lynn, Norfolk: The South Porch*, Unpublished Churches Conservation Trust Report (2014)

fine fifteenth century painted pulpit. The pulpit is made up of six main panels, four painted with images of the Latin doctors of the church, and one each of the donor John (Johannes) Godalle and his wife Katherine. Although little is known of Godalle with certainty it is believed that he was a wealthy local merchant who made his fortune in maritime trade.[18] Whatever the case, and there are local stories of his involvement in less legitimate maritime activities, he amassed enough wealth to be able to donate a not inconsiderable sum for the creation of a top quality piece of church ornament – only for it to be subsequently defaced with graffiti.

The graffiti that occurs on the pulpit at Burham Norton is very limited in nature, in the fact that it only includes ship graffiti, and these inscriptions are only to be found on a single panel – that of the merchant and donor John Godalle. Scored across the paintwork that depicts his pleated merchant's gown are a number of crude depictions of ships. Whilst it may be that it was the actual image of Goldalle, and his association with the sea, that encouraged the placement of the graffiti exactly there, perhaps suggesting a highly localised and small-scale cult, it may also be related to the positioning of the actual panel on the pulpit itself. Although the pulpit is today located on the north side of the chancel arch, leaving the panel containing the image of Goldalle obliquely facing the rood screen, recent works in the body of the church indicated that this wasn't its original position. Works undertaken in the area of the more modern pulpit uncovered the original footings for the medieval pulpit, which would have been located on the south side of the chancel arch. When the pulpit had been in this position it would have left the image of Goldalle, and the ship graffiti, directly facing the side altar at the east end of the south aisle – in just the same manner as the ship graffiti seen only a few miles away at Blakeney. There are other crude examples of ship graffiti to be found at Burnham Norton, and all located on the south side of the chancel arch, again supporting the idea that the graffiti was related to a particular area, an area of enhanced spiritual value, within the church.

18 Pevsner, N. and Wilson, B., *The Buildings of England: Norfolk 2: North-West and South*, Yale University Press (1999) p.230

Some of the earliest datable examples of ship graffiti from an ecclesiastical setting are to be found a short distance from Blakeney in the church of St Margaret at Cley-next-the-Sea. St Margaret's has a complex building history. The church was largely rebuilt in magnificent style during the second quarter of the 14th century, leaving only the 13th century tower from an earlier structure, reflecting the settlement's growing wealth from the maritime trade that flowed through its port.[19]

In the 15th century the elaborate two storey south porch was added, regarded as one of the finest to survive anywhere in East Anglia. However, by the time the porch was complete the trade that had fuelled and funded the large scale rebuilding was already waning. As the port dried up so too did the wealth that it had brought to

A fine example of late medieval ship graffiti from the church of Cley-next-the-Sea, Norfolk. The high forecastle and rigging lines running to the rear of the vessel share marked similarities with manuscript depicitions of medieval cogs.

Cley and by the mid-16th century the two transepts were described as already being in a ruinous state and were walled off from the rest of the church. This general decline helped to ensure that the church was not subject to subsequent major rebuilding, leaving the vast majority of the 14th century church intact. Happily the church also escaped the attention of 18th and 19th century 'restorers', who often re-surfaced piers and repaired stonework, which would have obliterated evidence of early graffiti.

19 Hooton, J., *The Glaven Ports: A maritime History of Blakeney, Cley and Wiveton in North Norfolk*, Blakeney History Group (1996)

St Margaret's contains a vast array of diverse graffiti inscriptions, including apotropaic markings, textual inscriptions, faces and figures.[20] It also contains a great many detailed examples of ship graffiti, many of which are so precisely executed that it has been possible to identify and date the type of ships depicted. One particular graffito, located at the eastern end of the south arcade, shows an absolutely typical example of a mid-14th century cog; a type of cargo vessel that would have been a regular sight in the harbour located nearby. The detailed depiction of the fore- and aft-castles, the layout of the rigging and the hull profile make its identification unambiguous, and it appears most likely that it was created shortly after the arcade itself was constructed. Although there does appear to be a concentration of ship graffiti on the easternmost pier of the south arcade, as seen at Blakeney, there are a number of other examples scattered across the piers of the rest of the church. Whilst the eastern pier appears to be a focus for the graffiti the distribution pattern is by no means as clear and straightforward as that seen at Blakeney, Winchelsea and Burnham Norton. However, whilst it isn't possible to suggest exactly what form of spiritual activity the ship graffiti might be associated with, it is clear that it is associated with some form of devotional ritual.

A mile to the east of St Margaret's stands the equally imposing church of St Nicholas in the now shrunken coastal village of Salthouse. Here too the revenue generated by the North Sea trade brought prosperity. Although never truly one of the Glaven ports, the village was served by a separate river channel that linked it directly to Blakeney and the sea and for much of the later Middle Ages it too was a thriving port. Salthouse's church was one of the last along this stretch of coast to be significantly rebuilt during the great 15th century church construction boom, only being completed as late as 1503, and little except the tower remains of the earlier medieval church.[21] As a result all the earlier graffiti inscriptions that might have been present have been wiped away. However, despite not having been finished until the early years of the 16th century, Salthouse church is still full of ship graffiti. Indeed, it probably contains one of the largest single collections of ship graffiti recorded to date.

20 Champion, *Medieval Graffiti: the lost voices of England's churches*, pp.233–234

21 Pevsner, N. and Wilson, B., *The Buildings of England: Norfolk 1: Norwich and North East*, Yale University Press (1997) pp.655–656

The site now appears to contain in excess of 50 individual examples of ship graffiti and almost all of these are to be found on the rear of the original rood and parclose screens. However, Salthouse church has suffered much at the hands of restorers and renovators who have been involved in several re-orderings of the church interior, and the screens have been much mutilated and moved throughout the centuries. Today the bulk of the rood screen is located towards the western end of the nave, with the parclose screens having been deconstructed to form the back of the choir stalls at the east end. A further fragment of four panels of rood screen

A collection of post-medieval examples of ship graffiti cut through the pigment on the rear of the rood screen at Salthouse church, Norfolk.

is also located in the south aisle, but its relationship to the larger sections located at the western end of the nave remains unclear. The re-ordering of the screens is recorded as having taken place as late as the 18th century and the evidence from the screens themselves suggest that the majority of the ship graffiti was applied prior to the re-ordering. This is particularly clear on the rear of the rood screen. Originally the rear of the screen had some form of benches or pews attached to them for support. As a result the original pigment covered only the upper sections of the screen, with the area that would have been beneath the benches left as bare wood. It is clear that all the examples of ship graffiti were cut through or into this pigment and not into the area beneath where the benches would have been attached.

The vast majority of the ships found at Salthouse are very different from the examples found a few miles away at Cley. The vessels depicted here are shown as having much more complex designs, with multiple masts, elaborate sterns and banners flying. Those that contain datable features suggest that they were created from the late sixteenth century onwards, until the eighteenth century relocation of the rood screen. Other smaller and simpler examples found within the church, particularly those found on the backs of the choir stalls, may well post date even the 18th century, suggesting that the practice of ship graffiti continued on within Salthouse church long after it appears to have ended in the neighbouring churches. Whether this continuation was linked to devotional and ritual practice is unclear. Given the sheer quantity of ship graffiti found within the building, and the fact that some examples appear to date from very recent centuries, if not recent decades, it would appear unlikely. With the presence of graffiti inscriptions already recognised as attracting further graffiti inscriptions, it can be suggested that whilst the end result at Salthouse may look identical, the motivation of those creating the ship graffiti in the 16th century and those creating the ship graffiti in the 19th century were quite different. Whilst such a suggestion is, by its very nature, impossible to prove it must be noted that the later inscriptions do not appear to follow any specific distribution pattern, excepting that they appear to favour more hidden away locations than the earlier inscriptions, and are accompanied by 'memorial' and 'souvenir' graffiti far more typical of the period, suggesting a far more clandestine approach to their creation. As has been recognised previously, the earlier devotional and ritual ship graffiti required no such clandestine approach, being located in many of the most prominent and obvious positions within the church.

Conclusions

It is clear that many of the better examples of ship graffiti to be found on the walls of our churches can tell us a very great deal. In the first instance they can tell us about the type of ships that operated locally throughout the later Middle Ages. The highly detailed examples, such as the cog from Cley, can also offer insights and tantalising hints concerning construction techniques and the manner in which these vessels were rigged and operated. Taken as a whole, the ship graffiti collections can also help to emphasis the links between local communities and the maritime trade of the medieval world. However, the distribution patterns now being recognised at a number of churches are suggesting that the images might be able to tell us far more than just the technical details of ships and shipping.

So are these many hundreds of images of medieval ships simply the doodling of bored choir boys, or do they represent something more? Something meaningful? The evidence from the church walls would appear to suggest that they are. These numerous images of ships would appear to be something different from what they might at first appear to show. Most of them are most certainly not just idle scratchings, and relate instead to the unbroken links between coastal communities and the sea. However, rather than simply memorialising the trade that took place across East Anglia with continental Europe, many of them appear to have been created as a direct result of the trade itself, and the many thousands of people that it involved. They are not simply images of the ships that were involved in such commerce, but were actually visualisations of faith and hope for those whose lives were so closely linked to the sea. The examples from Blakeney, Winchelsea and Burnham Norton all suggest a clear link between the creation of the images and areas of the church, such as the side altar, that were deemed to have been spiritually significant. Even leaving aside the tantalising suggestion that such ship images may be associated with either local cults, or a wider cult of St Nicholas, it is clear that the ship graffiti had a spiritual function in much the same manner as the votive church ships that once commonly hung in hundreds of English churches.

It is also clear that our traditional concepts of graffiti, as something produced illicitly in hidden away darkened corners, cannot be applied to these inscriptions. Although today these inscriptions are often difficult to make out, being visible sometimes only under certain light conditions, that wasn't the case for most of them when they were first created. Most churches during the Middle Ages were, almost without exception, covered in wall paintings.[22] Although the main paintings of the saints and angels would have been located high on the walls, away from the inevitable damp, even the lower sections of the walls and pillars, where the graffiti is most usually to be found, were covered in pigment. Examination of surviving pigment at churches such as Blakeney and Weston Longville has shown that these areas could be

22 Rosewell, R., *Medieval Wall Paintings in English and Welsh Churches*, Boydell (2009)

painted a wide variety of colours, including red ochres, yellow ochres and black — and the graffiti would have been scratched through these layers of pigment to reveal the pale stone beneath. The result would have been that the graffiti inscriptions, far from being hidden away and difficult to see, would have been one of the most obvious things you saw as you entered the church.

The fact that these graffiti inscriptions were actually highly visible within the church interior can change the way we view their function and acceptability to the local church authorities. To return to the little

ships of Blakeney church, by considering the medieval paint scheme of the church we can now visualise the pillar opposite the side altar in the south aisle in an entirely different way. At the time the ship graffiti was cut into the stonework we know that the pier was painted a deep red ochre, and fragments of pigment can still be seen in recesses and undercuts to this day. The graffiti cut through this paintwork to expose the creamy coloured stone beneath, leaving the whole

A tentative reconstruction of how the graffiti inscriptions would have appeared within the late medieval church setting, cutting through the pigment to reveal the pale stone beneath.

pier looking as though it was covered in a fleet of small white ships sailing across a deep red ocean. We also know that the ship images were created over a period of one or two centuries, and the fact that each one respects the space of the others around it indicates that the earlier ships were still clearly visible when the later ones were inscribed. Had the images been regarded as destructive or unwelcome then, at any point within those two centuries, the vicar or churchwardens could have had them either removed or covered over. That this didn't happen, as evidenced by the fact that the earlier inscriptions were still clearly visible when the later ones were made, strongly indicates that the inscriptions were both accepted and acceptable. They were not regarded as vandalism by the local church authorities, but as legitimate and highly visible expressions of faith and piety.

These ship images that adorn the walls quite clearly resulted from, and were linked to, acts of devotion on the part of the medieval congregation. In many cases they were, put simply, prayers made solid in stone. The question that must then be asked is exactly what was the nature of this prayer? Were these images an act of thanksgiving for a voyage already safely completed, much like many of the ex-voto items presented to medieval shrines, or were they perhaps a prayer for safe passage on a voyage not yet undertaken? More intriguingly, it has been suggested that, at a number of sites, some of the ship images appear to show clear damage to their masts and rigging, and that perhaps each of these images represents a ship that was long overdue; a vessel that just never made it home again? Without further documentary or archaeological evidence the exact function and meaning of these little ships that litter the walls of our churches may never be known. However, it is clear that they form, even after over five centuries, a direct and tangible link to the importance that seafaring, and trade, played in the lives and livelihoods of medieval East Anglians.

Reluctant Warriors? Arming a Hanseatic Cog and its Crew

David Nicolle

The Hanse was a commercial association in which politics and military matters only came to the fore as a means of protecting the Hanse's trading network. The Hanse was often also viewed with jealous or predatory eyes by several neighbouring states, most notably by Denmark. As a result the Hanseatic towns had to defend themselves, their ships, their trading outposts and their allies. The Hanse consequently developed several advanced military and naval systems while using its considerable wealth to obtain modern military equipment though remaining surprisingly conservative when it came to specifically maritime technology.

A feudal military structure was in place along the eastern marches of the German Empire by the 13th century, but its bonds were looser than the military structures seen elsewhere in Germany. Consequently feudal musters were already being supplemented with mercenaries in this region. Another feature of medieval German warfare was that many of the surviving written accounts were by townsmen. They tended to be more sympathetic to troops of non-noble status than were the chroniclers of France or England whose patrons were almost invariably from the senior aristocracy. Furthermore, significant military and naval contingents themselves came from the towns. This was particularly notable during various north German struggles against Denmark when the cities that became the Hanseatic League provided large numbers of troops.

In northern Germany, as elsewhere in Europe, such urban fighting forces were often based upon town quarters and guild structures. The latter ranged from the wealthy guilds of politically powerful merchants to those of quite humble craftsmen. Within the Hanseatic cities successful merchants were, in practical terms, only really distinguished from the ruling élite or patriciate by their relatively lesser wealth. Furthermore, it was from the wealthiest merchants that the patriciate itself drew new members. Meanwhile skilled craftsmen could, by the late 14th century, form over half the male inhabitants of a trading city. In Lübeck they were, for example, 43% of the population. Beneath them in status and wealth were those who lacked a recognised 'craft skill', who owned no property, were aged or sick or were orphans. Meanwhile, the cities themselves were governed by councils whose members were largely drawn from the urban patriciate. These councils were also taking over duties that had previously been undertaken by feudal lords. These included responsibility for defending their city against neighbouring principalities which often still claimed lordship over the city in question. The resulting clashes between urban and princely power centres were frequent, sometimes bloody but generally resulted in the cities extending their own authority over the surrounding countryside.

Mid- to late 14th century dagger found in the kogge from the river Weser.

In the early days German forces had been subject to a *waffenrecht* or law which banned peasants from using a lance or sword, wear armour or ride a warhorse. This effectively left such men only with only a bow and a dagger. The *waffenrecht* was in fact intended to preserve the military dominance of the knightly élite but it notably failed to do so, especially when mercenaries and territorial levies adopted crossbows. Nevertheless, restrictions on the bearing of arms remained in law, though it was at the same time accepted that merchants needed to be properly armed when travelling; this being a period when 'law and order' in a modern sense was notably lacking. For example, a clause in the Peace of Stralsund of 1370 illustrated a resulting and perhaps typical compromise, declaring that only while passing between his ship and his lodgings was a maritime merchant allowed to carry weapons. If otherwise found armed on land he would have to pay a fine.

In the early days German urban militias were led into battle by their towns' mayors. During the 13th century Baltic or 'Northern' crusades, however, large numbers of the same men went on crusade. In 1246 some of those who fought alongside the Teutonic Knights in Prussia were referred to as *juvenes Lubicenses*, 'young men of Lübeck'. In fact Lübeck played such a leading role in these campaigns that the Papacy offered indulgences to those who supported the crusade rather than necessarily taking an active combat role themselves. Many of these individuals are also known to have grown rich in the process, providing transport, supplies, food or other such essential services.

Lübeck was certainly not alone in having a highly effective military administration. Such cities were divided into quarters, each usually having a gate through the city or town's outer defensive wall. Each of the parishes within these fortifications raised a militia unit of local parishoners or citizens, the unit itself being under a *viertelmeister* 'quarter-master' appointed by the city council. He was normally assisted by other officers, plus a trumpeter and a guard to man that quarter's watchtower. Fortifications were meanwhile maintained through local taxes, as were drill squares and shooting ranges where militiamen would practise their skills, most notably with the crossbow.

From the 13th century onwards, the main elements within German urban militias, naturally including those of the militarily effective Hanseatic League, were armoured men equipped and trained for close combat, both as cavalry or as infantry, plus the crossbowmen who formed a separate force. In fact crossbows became characteristic of Hanseatic armies. Citizens kept their military equipment at home, ready to promptly obey a military summons. Those wealthy enough to serve as cavalry were organised in the same *gleven* system as seen in

'The army Knes (Prince) Henry of the Obotrites', carrying the medieval banners of Mecklenburg and Schwerin, in the Rhyming Chronicle of Mecklenburg by Ernst von Kirchberg, c.1378 .

medieval German feudal and mercenary armies. This was comparable to the *lances* of France and Italy. At first such a unit generally consisted of a knight or man-at-arms plus three armoured sergeants, but later it consisted either of the man-at-arms plus lightly armed servants, or of three hired mercenaries. One of the latter would have been an armoured cavalryman, the second being a light cavalryman or mounted crossbowman and the third a servant or page.

Meanwhile, the better armed burghers were still fighting as active soldiers in the late 14th century, by which time many towns also employed a *büchsenmeister* or master gunner. Urban militia contingents supposedly dressed in their city's own colours and marched behind

Carriage with an armed escort, panel-painting, early to mid-15th century, in situ Heiligen-Geist Hospital in Lübeck.

their own banners. Many German cities also had a 'banner waggon' comparable to the better-known Italian *carroccio*. Perhaps even more importantly, these north German urban armies clearly had effective logistical support.

Remarkable as it was, this system did not, of course, always work perfectly. Political tensions persisted and the leaders of a city sometimes had to make a choice between external security and internal stability. If dissident groups within a city were disarmed, the city would lose vital troops, but if these dissidents remained armed they might pose a security risk. So some Hanseatic cities like 14th century Cologne took drastic action by stripping their militias of useful fighting men.

Amongst neighbouring territorial princes the Count of Holstein was supported by a *marshal* and a *constable* — the two most senior military ranks below that of the ruler himself in a system seen across virtually all of medieval western and central Europe. He was also supported by urban burghers, including those of some Hanse towns, while rural militiamen formed the majority of the Holstein's 13th–14th century territorial levies. The organisation of Holstein's armies was also the same as that seen elsewhere, with units known as *banieren* or *conroten* consisting of around 20 cavalrymen. The Latin term *turma* probably meant the same for cavalry but was also used for infantry units. The numbers of available knights was, however, only in the hundreds, with the figure of 400 commonly being mentioned. On the other hand, these knights were supported by squires and servants including 'shield boys' who did not normally fight but looked after the fighting men's horses.

The militias were more numerous. When levies were summoned from farming communities they assembled at their local parish churches. Then, after spiritual encouragement from the parish priest, these rural militiamen went off to the Count of Holstein's designated muster area. In many parts of early 15th century Germany such levies were summoned on the basis of households; for example, in 1421 one man was demanded from every ten such households. Nevertheless, the effectiveness of non-urban militias varied considerably. On one hand the coastal Frisians had a high fighting and naval reputation. Indeed their somewhat isolated homeland was never fully feudalized. Regarded by outsiders as an almost free people, these Frisians owed their primary loyalty to their local church leaders, and the men were certainly welcome on crusade, especially during the first half of the 13th century. Nevertheless, few Frisians were mounted and their traditional weapon seemed rather archaic, being a short spear or javelin. Reliance upon infantry was also a feature of Dithmarschen rural levies from the most northerly Frisian communities, though their traditional or preferred weapon was a long-hafted axe.

Legally unfree but nevertheless militarily élite *ministeriales* were particularly characteristic of medieval Germany, though they were also found in some other parts of Europe. The majority inhabited rural castles while some lived in towns, having been installed there by feudal lords to supervise potentially troublesome urban populations. Urban *ministeriales* were particularly important in the forces of 13th century Cologne, but much less is known concerning the role of *ministeriales* in northern German towns along the Baltic coast, including those of what became the Hanseatic League.

Militarily more important for the emerging Hanseatic cities were mercenaries. Some towns soon hired *aüssoldner* 'pensioners' to offset the power of local aristocracies but these troops, including cavalry, were only paid half wages in peacetime. Generally speaking the autonomous princes of northern Germany relied less upon mercenaries than did the cities, although the Teutonic Knights who ruled Prussia were a notable exception. Nevertheless, paid troops would soon play a significant role in 14th century Holstein. Towards the end of the 13th century it was already customary for Holsteiner knights to serve Lübeck but they unfortunately earned a reputation for disturbing the peace and therefore had to be removed from the lists of permanently employed troops. Instead, from the mid-14th century onwards, Holstein knights were employed by Lübeck and others as mercenaries within units of from four to ten men, including crossbowmen. Documentary evidence suggest that members of the same family commonly served together, which could result in knightly families suffering considerable loss after a bloody defeat. During the mid-14th century Lübeck's mercenary knights tended to enlist in small groups and were paid through their leader. At the same time contracts between cities like Lübeck and

Detail of a sequence of wall-paintings illustrating the story of the Emperor Heraclius, late 12th or early 13th century, in Brunswick cathedral.

these knightly mercenaries usually agreed that such men would not be expected to fight against their own feudal lords.

Less is known about lower status mercenaries and although these men could earn considerable wealth, they were rarely promoted into the aristocracy. For the Hanse towns, most mercenary infantry were recruited from Hanover, Westphalia, Thuringia and Saxony. Mercenary crossbowmen would, in fact, largely replace local militia crossbowmen by the end of the 14th century and by the end of the medieval period Hanseatic towns were enlisting mercenaries for garrison duty even in times of peace. A city council would give a mercenary leader a letter of authority to enlist recruits, along with a date and place of muster for himself and his troops, this usually being a port. Recruits were also given travel expenses in advance to help them reach the muster point and they would similarly be provided with money for their journey home when paid off.

The regularly paid 'city servants' of Hanseatic cities were intended to maintain law and order rather than to form an army. Their pay varied, but in Stralsund in 1360 a mounted 'city servant' received 15 marks annually. Even in peacetime military expenditure accounted for over 80% of Cologne's civic spending in 1379. In 1437 Rostock the sum similarly stood between 76% and 80%. Full-scale naval or land campaigns were even more costly, Hanseatic expeditions being financed by taxes levied in the cities and by tariffs imposed on trade.

Military equipment was, of course, a major expenditure and armour became more expensive as it grew more sophisticated. The coat-of-plates, for example,

Wall-painting of St George with the Virgin & Child, mid-14 century story of the Emperor Heraclius, late 12th or early 13th century in Lübeck cathedral.

had probably first been seen in Germany in the mid-13th century. This initially consisted of large plates of iron or hardened leather attached to an outer layer of sturdy cloth. Thereafter the plates generally became smaller and more numerous as the armour became more flexible and easier to wear. In fact the coat-of-plates proved notably effective against archery. Meanwhile the standard of equipment expected of militiamen varied between cities but as such expectations increased, so did cost.

The major role of crossbows in Baltic warfare gave a significant advantage to Germans and Scandinavians over the pagan peoples of the southern and eastern Baltic from the later 12th century onwards. By that time most

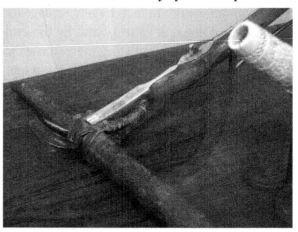

Crossbow with a composite bowstave, German, late 15th century, Deutsches Historisches Museum, Berlin.

north German crossbows had bowstaves of composite construction, made in essentially the same manner as Middle Eastern Islamic crossbows though being very different to the composite construction of oriental hand-held bows. Nevertheless the incorporation of whalebone in composite crossbow staves would be a distinctly northern concept. Fragments and virtually complete crossbows dating from the first half of the 14th century have been found in several parts of northern Europe and Scandinavia. One example from Lübeck incorporates a reinforced groove made of antler horn in which the bolt or arrow sat. A similar crossbow from Hanseatic Cologne dates from around 1400 and both weapons have composite bowstaves.

Large, non-portable 'wall crossbows' could be mounted on a frame or cart for open warfare though the main role was in siege warfare. The variety of crossbows used in 14th century Germany is highlighted by their terminology and the differing methods used to span or draw back their powerful bows. For example, in 1307 and 1308 Hamburg purchased ten *balistas stegerepas* which were normal stirrup crossbows, plus ten *balistas dorsales* or 'back crossbows'. The latter may have been spanned with a *croc* or hook which, in German, was often corrupted to *rück* which could also mean the back, or they may have been spanned by an early form of so-called 'goat's foot' lever which came into use during the 14th century.

Crossbow bolts included those with tanged or with socketed heads, and were primarily designed to penetrate armour. There were also significant developments during the 14th century, as when Frankfurt-am-Main ordered that many crossbows be modernised and their bolts or arrows shortened. The resulting short bolt with its steel head could penetrate virtually any armour at close range. Furthermore, finds from a wrecked *kogge* at Kalmar include crossbow bolts with spiral fletching which made the missiles revolve in flight to achieve a degree of accuracy not reached by guns until the introduction of rifling. Unlike his traditional rival, the so-called longbowman, a trained crossbowman relied upon the power and accuracy of his shot rather than the speed of his shooting and the weight of his arrow.

It is also worth noting that the supposedly poor rate of shooting of crossbows, almost universally accepted by military historians, may be exaggerated. Unlike an ordinary archer, a crossbowman normally worked with a second man who spanned and perhaps also loaded the weapon. As an infantry team they could achieve a much faster 'rate of fire' than if the crossbowman operated alone. Furthermore the shooter avoided tiring his arms by spanning and respanning his weapon. Instead he could concentrate on accuracy, which was always the crossbow's great advantage.

In medieval northern and western Germany, including virtually all members of the Hanseatic League, the process of attaching bolt-heads to bolt shafts was called *sticken*; the craftsman who did this job being known as a *pilsticker*. He also manufactured the flighted shafts. On campaign enormous quantities of such bolts were carried in casks; an army's or fleet's munitions being assessed in terms of casks rather than the missiles themselves. Thus in northern Germany and Denmark it was reckoned that a cast or keg contained 800 bolts.

The resale of captured military equipment, or that retrieved from a battlefield, was probably as common in northern Europe as it certainly was in southern Europe. Travelling merchants are likely to have done a brisk trade in such items at trading fairs in times of crisis. However, wealthy cities like those of the Hanseatic League also encouraged weapons makers to settle within their own walls, especially the highly skilled craftsmen who made or repaired crossbows. For example, guilds of crossbowmakers are known to have existed in 14th and 15th century Lübeck, as they did elsewhere, and they included a heirarchy of masters, journeymen and apprentices. Such guilds had strict rules governing the quality of raw materials, a requirement that completed crossbows be marked so their maker could be identified, and official permission for these craftsmen to work on religious holidays because their work was so important.

Master craftsmen were prohibited from enticing workers away from other masters while discipline within the guild was ensured by punishments which included fines payable to the guild or to the city. An alternative sanction was to insist than on offender supply wax for the candles used in churches, which highlighted the important religious underpinning of these crafts guilds. German cities similarly had their own official, full-time crossbow maker whose job was to make a certain number of weapons each year. Conditions of employment varied but the Hanseatic city of Hamburg can be taken as an example. Here, from the start of the 14th century, the city's own *balistarius*, *balistifex*, or *armborstmakere* had to produce four weapons a year, being paid extra for any additional he could make.

Crossbowmen were not, of course, the only foot soldiers — militiamen or mercenaries — to be raised by the cities and towns of the Hanseatic League. In fact it has been suggested that the League played a leading role in the rise and development of well trained, cohesive infantry formations in northern Germany. This phenomenon was also seen in the highly urbanised Rhineland, and as a result the period from the mid-14th century through the 15th century became what is called the *volkssöldnertum* during which the dominance of the knight was reduced by the increasing effectiveness of commoners fighting on foot.

There is not the same amount of contemporary written information about the use of infantry weapons as there is for cavalry. Nevertheless, surviving weapons and armour, as well as the evidence of pictorial sources, make it clear that protection for the hands and head was a primary concern. Some pole-arms or staff weapons demanded great skill from the individual foot soldier and considerable cohesion as well as discipline within infantry formations. A primary function of such long hafted weapons was to reach a man on horseback, and to break or penetrate his armour. In contrast, shorter pole-arms were of more use against an opponent on foot. Experimental archaeologists claim to have identified different combat actions for use when advancing or when in a static defensive posture, or when fighting

Soldiers at 'The Passion', Triptych of the Kanonischen Tageszeiten, first half of the 15th century, Lübeck cathedral.

behind field fortifications. Many of these same actions would also have been useful in naval warfare where boarding remained the primary tactic. Another set of infantry skills concerned short swords, axes and short spears which were still used with shields or small bucklers in much of the German Empire. These, however, were primarily for closer and more mobile combat, again inevitably including naval warfare.

Maritime Warfare c.1250–c.1425

Sailors were mostly drawn from fishermen, day-labourers and rural peasantry. Their well-being and their lives might be in the hands of merchants and the city authorities, but their wages were predictable and they were allowed to take part in trading, which, with luck, could make families prosperous. The wages themselves were graduated according to skills and duties aboard ship; a ship's carpenter being highly paid, along with gunners and senior crewmen with authority over others. Yet even ordinary sailors enjoyed respect because they were recognised as being vital for the prosperity and security of Hanseatic towns.

Marine troops who defended ships and convoys were recruited from the towns involved, usually from the urban militia. All able-bodied citizens could theoretically be called upon to defend a city's ships as well as a city's walls. Even though during the 13th and 14th centuries Hamburg, Rostock and others had to employ naval mercenaries, the Hanseatic League became renowned for providing its own vessals with marine infantry consisting of free *knechte* or mercenaries. Some were probably drawn from the agreed contingents maintained by all Hanseatic member cities and were paid from funds provided by the League.

Siege Warfare & Firearms

Hanseatic forces took part in many sieges; one such being the Hanseatic siege of Stockholm Castle in 1395. The forces involved were agreed during a *Hansetag* or meeting of city representatives on 12th July that year. Here it was arranged that Prussian towns were to send 41 squires and 30 crossbowmen, while Toruń also supplied a crossbow-maker and, like Elbing and Danzig, a crossbow windlass, four 'benders' to enable the crossbows to be strung, three crossbow strings and ten windlass-spanned crossbows. Every crossbowman in the Prussian contingent must have 60 good quality *getulleter* 'socketted' crossbow bolts. Furthermore, Toruń, Gdańsk and Elbing must each send two kegs or barrels of bolts, those from Toruń consisting of one keg of *getullet* socketed and one keg of *gesticket* 'stuck' or tanged bolts.

The crossbows used in the Baltic region ranged from small weapons to the large and virtually static *bankarmbrüste* and *wallarmbrüste* which became widespread during the 15th century. A particularly interesting example of such a weapons with a composite bowstave 1.62 metres long is preserved in the Castle Museum in Quedlinburg in Saxony-Anhalt. It was captured by Quedlinburg's militia from the opposing castle of Gersdorf during the later 1330s. The bowstave is still attached to a mount made of oak from southern Lower Saxony while the internal structure of the bowstave consists of horn and sinew covered by parchment. Even more remarkably, the loft of the castle of Quedlinburg was also found to contain a virtually unique spanning mechanism, though not associated with this particular crossbow. It looks like a long wooden box, was operated with a rope and would have had some sort of windlass which is now unfortunately missing.

Small guns were certainly being used in the Baltic region by the second half of the 14th century. However, the Hanseatic cities in western Germany had such weapons

Powder chamber for a cannon, 15th century, Museum Holstentor, Lübeck.

even earlier and some Saxon towns had guns by at least the 1340s. The only real advantage that these early small-bore guns, operated by one or two men, had over crossbows was their greater armour penetration. Otherwise they remained expensive and unreliable, though as gunpowder got cheaper and guns more accurate with long rather than short, stubby barrels, their popularity would rapidly increase. Where larger guns were concerned, a proper artillery train required a great deal of money and a well-ordered government; both of these being notable features of the leading Hanseatic towns. These cities were in turn keen to prevent guns reaching their too often politically unreliable princely neighbours. Such concerns are reflected in a Saxon ballad of the 1340s, referring to a struggle between the Hanseatic city of Magdeburg and an alliance of princes — a struggle which ended with the princes' defeat:

Give ear to me, you princes high,
For I advise you faithfully
To keep the town as your ally
They have such good artillery
With guns that shoot so rapidly.

The first mention of a gun in Lübeck is found in a reference to a *vüerschütte* in 1352. Thereafter Lübeck led the Baltic Hanseatic cities in such matters, despite technical difficulties which could lead to disaster. For example, in 1360 the gunpowder stored in the cellars of Lübeck's town hall exploded, destroying this very important building. By the 15th century all major Hanseatic cities had guns and their use became quite sophisticated. During the Duke of Burgundy's siege of Cologne in 1474–5, for example, written messages were exchanged between the inhabitants and a newly arrived relief army; these being shot over the heads of the surrounding besiegers in *fusées* which were probably empty incendiary missiles.

Even more significant for the Hanseatic League was the use of guns at sea, the first reference being in 1384. Next year Wulf Wulflam of Stralsund used six *donnerbüchsen* guns in combat against pirates. Initially the impact of guns was more moral than physical, most of the guns being small, anti-personnel weapons such as *schotbussen* which were placed on a ship's gunwales. During the 15th century shipboard artillery became heavier. Meanwhile powder and shot became part of the normal defensive equipment on board large merchant ships. Even so guns were still not powerful enough to sink an enemy vessel.

The manufacture of guns and gunpowder was virtually confined to larger cities, production in Lübeck reportedly increasing significantly in the 1360s during a major struggle against Denmark. This industry was strategically so sensitive that in 1384 the Hanse banned the manufacture of guns for foreigners. A year later Rostock and its Hanseatic neighbours declared that 'in no town should guns be cast for those who are resident outside the towns'. Skilled gunners were nevertheless offering themselves as highly paid mercenaries in the late 14th century in several Hanseatic cities, including Hamburg and Lübeck. Some of these men were natives of neighbouring Holstein. They, or perhaps other specialists, also made gunpowder and by the

15th century the best paid, most prestigious and sometimes permanent job in this field was that of a city's 'gun master'.

Crusaders in the Hanseatic world: the 1390 expedition from Boston and the 1392 expedition from Kings Lynn

Andrew Hoyle

Mention the crusades to most people and they will think of Richard the Lion Heart and the fight for the Holy Land. A few will have heard of the Reconquest of Spain under Ferdinand and Isabella. The Baltic crusades however often meet with incomprehension and quizzical doubt that somewhere so far removed from Jerusalem could be termed a 'crusade'.

Within the towns of Boston and Kings Lynn the two crusading expeditions which started from these Wash ports have been almost entirely forgotten. Occasional references crop up in the footnotes of academic works, but locally the memory has gone. The purpose of this account is to help revive awareness of Boston and King's Lynn's medieval interaction with the Hanseatic League's greatest regional member.

The relative obscurity of the Baltic crusades is undeserved. The Baltic wars were not only crusades in the fullest sense of the word, but occupied a significant position within the medieval imagination. Fulfilling all the legal criteria for crusade warfare, they took place against a background of an astonishing flowering of high chivalric culture at the Prussian courts that was worthy of King Arthur and his knights.

The two crusading expeditions led by Henry earl of Derby (later King Henry IV) in 1390 from Boston and 1392 from Kings Lynn can be reconstructed in great detail. This is due to the meticulous accounts kept by his 'Treasurer for War', Richard de Kyngston, archdeacon of Hereford, who accompanied Henry on both expeditions. The accounts were jotted down at the time on notes, slips and small rolls of parchment, and made up upon return to England. Preserved in the archives of the royal household, they were later transferred to the Public Record Office, translated in the mid-19th century and printed by the Camden Society with an excellent commentary by Lucy Toulmin Smith (which has provided the basis for much of this account).

Henry of Derby's crusades are mentioned in other medieval sources, in particular the *Ypodigma Neustriae* of the St Albans monk Thomas Walsingham and the chronicle of John Capgrave, an Augustinian friar at Kings Lynn. Prussian sources are also important, including the chronicle *Chronik des Landes Preussen* kept by John of Posilge, a priest at Eilau; as well as the chronicle *Scriptores rerum Prussicarum*.

Before we can discuss in detail the 1390 expedition we should pose a few questions: What were the crusades? Who were the Teutonic Knights? Who was Henry of Derby?

What were the crusades?

The crusades were papally approved Holy Wars against Christendom's internal and external enemies. There were many crusades which took place across several centuries. There were crusades not just to the Holy Land but to north Africa and Egypt, within Spain, and to the eastern Baltic lands Even the 1588 Armada has been portrayed in crusading terms. Internal crusades were also launched against heretics, notably the Albigensian crusade in Provence. The crusading era extended from 1095 into the 18th century. Within the medieval period the impact of crusading ideology on social, religious and intellectual activity was immense.

There has been over the years a great deal of ambiguous talk about crusaders and crusading. However, the late Professor Jonathan Riley-

Smith has proved that a crusade had a very precise legal definition and encompassed three key aspects: a crusade must be declared by the pope in defence of Christian lands or people; crusaders must take a vow to perform military service on the crusade; in return they receive an indulgence to forgive their sins. Unless these qualifications are met an expedition cannot be called a crusade.

While on crusade the crusaders were granted the same privileges and support as pilgrims (financial support, legal immunity, practical support in terms of food and shelter etc.), therefore it is accurate to think of a crusade as a military pilgrimage.

At the end of the crusade the crusader returned to normal life — or went on another crusade.

Who were the Teutonic Knights?

One of the three great crusading orders of knighthood, the Teutonic Knights, were formed by the citizens of Bremen and Lübeck in 1187. As well as running their own hospital in Jerusalem, the knights protected

pilgrims in the Holy Land. The formal name of the order was The Order of Brothers of the German House of Saint Mary in Jerusalem.

A distinction needs to be made between the Teutonic knights, and the bulk of the crusading armies. It is important to realise that the Teutonic Knights were fighting monks, not crusaders. Unlike other

A grand-master of the Teutonic knights — note the black cross and the elaborate horned helmet. Meister des Codex Manesse (Grundstockmaler).

crusaders the Teutonic knights were permanently engaged in the defence of Christendom. They lived in a religious community and followed the Augustinian Rule. After the fall of Jerusalem 1187 the order was re-founded in Acre in 1190.

In 1230 they were asked by Pope Gregory IX to undertake a crusade against the pagan Prussians, a Slavic tribe that was raiding the eastern border of the Holy Roman Empire. So successful were the knights that they eventually controlled the whole of Prussia and set up their own quasi-independent state. This was an event that was to have profound implications for European and world history and to resonate for centuries to come.

After the fall of Acre in 1291 the Teutonic Knights moved their headquarters first to Venice and then to Marienburg (Malbork) on the river Vistula. Eastward expansion continued, and the knights moved into Pomerania and along the Baltic coast, linking up and absorbing other smaller knightly orders. The scale of their ambitions is indicated by the fact that the bishopric of Marienburg had no eastern border — expansion was theoretically infinite, to the end of the earth.

The Teutonic Knights were part of the Hanseatic League and were the only regional members of the League. Danzig (Gdansk) was a Teutonic knights' port and had strong links with Boston, Lynn, Hull and York. As the Teutonic Knights moved eastwards the Hanseatic League expanded.

The Grand Commander of the Teutonic Knights lived at Marienburg, the Marshal at Königsberg (Kaliningrad) and the Grand Hospitaller at Elbing (Elblag) — all major Hanseatic ports. In theory the Grand Commander was a Prince of the

Marienburg Castle.

Holy Roman Empire and also nominally subject to the Pope and the King of Poland. In practice Prussia was an independent state.

At this point it is necessary to say a few words about later, anachronistic, views of the Teutonic Knights. This was not a Germans versus Slavs contest. The Teutonic Knights were not exclusively German — they spoke German but followed the international rule of the Augustinians and recruited throughout Europe. The Prussian population was originally ethnically Slav. Medieval society was feudal, not nationalistic and loyalty was to a lord, not to abstract ideas of nationalism. Later generations, particularly in the 20th century, distorted the medieval history of this region to suit an ideological agenda which is not justified by the history of the medieval period.

Henry of Derby

Henry, Earl of Derby, was the eldest son of John of Gaunt, Duke of Aquitaine and Lancaster and thus grandson to King Edward III. He was cousin to King Richard II and carried the Sword of Mercy or Curtana at Richard's coronation. In 1390 he was 25 years old, married to Mary de Bohun (at age 15) and had three sons. He was a great athlete accomplished at jousting and sword fighting, and one of the most important princes in England with an established reputation as a knight. He was a keen supporter of the crusades and went on two crusades to Prussia and the Baltic region.

Henry's household was modelled on the royal household, and included officers such as a steward, treasurer, controller, chamberlain, and chaplain. These officers followed him everywhere, even to war, fulfilling the feudal obligation for retainers to fight on behalf of their lord. Below the main officers there were an astonishingly varied and specialised range of household departments including the clerk of the kitchen, the marshall of the hall, butler, office of the saucery, office of the poultry, office of the scullery, clerk of the spicery (which included such delicacies as sugar, honey, almonds, dried fruits, even wafers made in Königsberg), office of the chaundry (responsible for soap, tallow, candles and torches), clerk of the buttery (provision of wine and beer in barrels), clerk of the pantry (in charge of baking bread, making pies, pastry cooks etc), clerk of the marshaley (hay, oats, horse shoes), and clerk of the great wardrobe.

As well as the administrative members of his household Henry also maintained a retinue of knights, esquires, valets, grooms, henchmen (young boys or wards being brought up in the household), pages and many servants. All of these men were bound personally to Henry by feudal oaths. The result was a household that could be transformed easily and relatively quickly into a fighting army.

Henry's base was Bolingbroke Castle in south Lincolnshire. He also had other properties including manors near Peterborough. On top of the income from his estates, Henry received ad hoc grants of money from his father, the Duke of Lancaster.

The 1390 Boston expedition

The background to Henry's expedition which sailed from Boston was the civil war in Lithuania that had broken out due to the union of Poland and Lithuania in 1386 when Uladislas, the son of Jagello, the Grand Duke of Lithuania, converted to Christianity and married Hedwig, Queen of Poland. This alliance was opposed by Jagello's cousin Vitold (Prince of Samogitia) who appealed to the Teutonic Knights for help. For complex geopolitical reasons the Teutonic Knights responded to this appeal and in 1390 planned an invasion of the Grand Duchy of Lithuania. They probably appealed for international help which came from England, France and the Low Countries. It was at this point that Henry of Derby decided to join the crusade and mustered his feudal force.

The English force

Henry's small army included 12 knights with their attendant esquires and valets. His household servants (from the stables, kitchen, buttery, pantry, poultry, falconry etc.) all joined the expedition and as well as carrying out logistical duties doubled as fighting men. Crucially, a troop of bowmen was also taken along. Priests staffed the earl's private chapel, and Lancaster Herald was included to perform ceremonial duties, announce the earl's presence to continental courts in north Germany, and to assert the earl's high status at every opportunity. The chronicler John of Posilge estimates Henry's army to be about 300, but this may include men recruited in Prussia.

Musicians

Payments to musicians feature surprisingly prominently in the accounts, indicating the high value placed on music in establishing social status. The army included six minstrels, a trumpeter, and five other musicians, and these seem to have acted as a kind of military band. Much as royalty is proclaimed today, one can imagine Henry's arrival at a German castle being announced with a fanfare of trumpets. The accounts reveal that many other musicians were employed locally in Prussia. The whole time Henry was on crusade he seems to have been surrounded by music, emphasising the chivalric nature of the expedition with its overtones of courtly romance.

Surnames in the Accounts

The prevalence of Lincolnshire placename surnames in the wage payments justifies the description of the force as a Lincolnshire army rather than a general English force. The officers, esquires and valets were drawn from the towns, manors and villages of the Bolingbroke demesne. The surnames can be divided into three parts: those names after a place (Willoughby, Bolingbroke, Melbourne); those named after an occupation (Baker, Cage Maker); those who have true surnames (Cudworth, Maunsell). The names recorded in the accounts would benefit from further study. Examples include Clerk of the Scullery Robert Spaigne (there is a Spain Lane in Boston, close to Henry's residence at Gysors Hall); Thomas Swinford (the accounts refer to horses brought from Kettlethorpe manor) and Lincolnshire knight ,Ralph Rochford.

Henry had originally planned to go on crusade to Tunis but the French king would not give him and his men permission to travel overland to Marseilles. At that point he returned from Calais and decided to go to Prussia and Lithuania. Two large vessels were commissioned, probably English but with German captains. One can speculate that these were almost certainly Hanseatic cogs, built of Baltic oak and with a single mast and square-rigged sail. Some of the largest cogs excavated have been up to 25 metres (80 feet) in length and 8 metres (25 feet) wide and could carry 200 tons, and therefore adequate for transporting a small armed force.

The ships were supplied as hulls and had to be fitted out – presumably at Boston, using local carpenters and shipwrights (one wonders whether beneath the silt and mud of the Haven the remains of the medieval ship yard still survive). As well as cabins for the lords and accommodation for the men, stables were added and a chapel. Perhaps the inclusion of a chapel underlines the religious nature of the expedition, since a crusade was simultaneously a military campaign and a pilgrimage.

While the ships were being fitted out other orders and commissions were being made. Richard de Kyngston, archdeacon of Hereford, was formally appointed Henry's 'Treasurer for War' on 6th May 1390 (another act that imitates and shadows the behaviour of the royal court and household). Large quantities of wine, beer and food were purchased, together with chattels and utensils. Horses and cattle were included in the inventory, possibly from Henry's estates in the Peterborough area. All these provisions were directed to Boston for loading onto the ships. The date for departure was set for the feast of St Margaret, 20th July.

The exact point of departure was a place called Chopehyr which was probably on a stretch of the Haven in Skirbeck.

The ships crossed the North Sea and passed by Copenhagen and into the Baltic, the voyage taking just over two weeks. We know that board games were played during this time as the accounts record payments of small wagers. On 8th August three men were landed on the Pomeranian coast at Leba, no doubt with orders to go ahead and prepare accommodation. Henry and a small party of retainers landed a little further along at Rixhoft (Rozewie). The first thing they did was have a meal – perhaps they had suffered from sea-sickness and were keen to get back on land. The ships went on to Danzig with Henry following on horseback.

Henry stayed in Danzig (Gdansk) from 10th to 13th August, at the house of 'Lord de Burser' – Professor Nigel Saul suggests this might be the English Lord Bouchier (see *For Honour and Fame* by Nigel Saul, Bodley Head 2011). The army disembarked and began to form up. Lancaster Herald took letters from Henry to the Grand Master of the Teutonic Knights at Marienburg (Malbork) – everywhere Henry went in Prussia heralds seem to have proceeded him to announce his arrival and to arrange food and lodging.

The English force moved forward and crossed the Vistula, proceeding towards Königsberg which they reached on 16th August. Thirteen carts were required to transport Henry's stores and armour. At the same time other stores and provisions were sent by water to Königsberg (Kaliningrad), conveyed in flat boats. In addition, 18 carts of provisions were diverted to the castle of Insterberg (Chernyakhovsk) for the post-crusade feasting. More cartloads of provisions were allocated to the after-party than were required for the actual military campaign (was this a logistical decision, or can we surmise that the partying aspect of the crusade was more important than the fighting?).

As Henry progressed through east Prussia he stayed at red-brick castles and fortified manor houses, each displaying in varying degrees the knightly and courtly culture of the north German gentry and aristocracy. Castle Cremitten, then Tapiau, then Norkitten — his hosts would have been familiar with crusaders on 'reise' (as the local crusades were called). On the whole his presence would have been welcomed as representing the forces of safety and aristocratic solidarity.

Eventually the English army approached the 'Wyldrenesse' or wilderness, a no-mans-land that divided Prussia from Lithuania. This was a great primeval forest that was almost impenetrable. It must have taken great courage for the Lincolnshire men to enter this dark forest.

On 24th August Henry's expedition crossed the Memel river and almost immediately encountered the Lithuanian forces. On Sunday 28th August there was a skirmish with the Lithuanians which the English claimed to have won, although Sir John Loudeham was killed in the fight. Three Lithuanian dukes, 11 boyars and 200 horses were captured — it is not surprising that these acquisitions were recorded in the accounts as they represented assets that had the potential to be converted into cash following the payment of ransoms.

Pushing further into the duchy of Lithuania, Henry and his army approached Vilnius, then as now the capital of Lithuania. Vilnius was strongly defended, with outer wooden defences and an inner hill-top stone citadel. There were three strongpoints in the city, the upper castle, the lower castle and the 'crooked' castle.

Three armies, including the English force, stormed the city which fell on 4th September 1390. Both the English and the German chronicles say that Henry of Derby's force was crucial to the capture of the city, the bowmen in particular being devastating. An English banner was the first to be planted, by a yeoman retainer of Lord Bouchier, on the walls of the captured city.

Vilnius was looted and burnt, and many prisoners were taken. But, despite a long siege, the inner hill-top fortress was not captured. Eventually sickness, a lack of gunpowder, and the onset of bad weather made the armies give up the siege, and Henry and his army returned to Königsberg which they reached on 20th October 1390.

Henry then went on a short pilgrimage to the church of St Katherine of Alexandria at Arnau, eight km. (five miles) from Königsberg. This red-brick church contains over 200 biblically-themed wall paintings dating from the fourteenth century, thus more or less contemporary with Henry's visit. One of the paintings (since destroyed but recorded in photographs) clearly shows a knight in the familiar horned helmet of the Teutonic order.

Fighting knights in the armour of the 14th century. Meister des Codex Manesse (Nachtragsmaler).

Henry spent four months in Königsberg, including Christmas and New Year. During this time he took part in a programme of jousting and hunting. Professor Jonathan Riley-Smith has suggested that the Teutonic Knights successfully developed a 'package tour' of chivalric magnificence to attract knights from all over Europe to take part in the Baltic crusades.

Over this holiday period Henry was continually presented with gifts including horses and hawks. The accounts also record the purchase of gifts for the local aristocracy, including fur robes, jewels, wax, spices, and linen. These exchanges of gifts would have been ritual and ceremonial occasions designed to demonstrate the high status of the English prince. Hire of musicians (in addition to the minstrels Henry brought with him from Lincolnshire) feature frequently in the accounts – indicating once more the use of music to underscore the prestige and eminence of the English visitors. Feasts were attended and given, including a feast at which roast peacocks were served. It is interesting to note that Chaucer's Knight in the *Canterbury Tales* is described as being placed at the head of the 'board' (the feasting table) at one of these post-crusade feasts.

One of the many duties of Lancaster Herald was to paint shields with coats of arms associated with the English army and to leave them

Ritual gift-giving was a significant element of courtly life. Meister des Codex Manesse (Grundstockmaler).

hanging in the castles where Henry stayed. Heraldic devices also featured in stained glass in churches (in *For Honour and Fame*, Professor Nigel Saul discusses proceedings in the Court of Chivalry which recount English heraldry preserved in churches and castles in Prussia, including in stained glass at a church in Königsberg).

In February 1391 Henry left Königsberg and arrived in Danzig, principal city of the Hanseatic League in Prussia, on 15th February. He stayed six weeks in the city as guest of the wealthy merchant Klaus Gottesknecht. Many of his party however were lodged at the castle-palace of the Bishop of Leslau just outside Danzig – the castle had to be fitted up at significant cost which indicates it was in a semi-derelict state.

Henry went on pilgrimages to four churches within Danzig and left offerings of money and gained 'indulgences'. He spent Easter (26th March 1391) in Danzig with festivities and gift-giving. It is worth mentioning that the accounts record several residents of Danzig with English names providing goods and services to Henry (eg John Bever) which suggests the English were very established in the city.

For the return home two ships were chartered under Prussian masters but with pilots from Boston. Carpenters created cabins for the men, stables for the animals and cages for the hawks. On 31st March 1391 Henry embarked for the voyage back to England. However instead of returning to Boston the ship landed at Hull (a town with strong Hanseatic connections). The most likely explanation for this diversion was the death on board ship of Henry Catour, who was probably from the south Yorkshire gentry family of the same name. Catour was buried at Hull and masses said for his soul, the accounts scrupulously recording the costs.

Henry then crossed from Hull to Barton and travelled overland, south to Bolingbroke Castle, stopping for supper at Caister en route. His baggage was sent by coastal vessels to Boston and then carted from Boston to Bolingbroke.

The 1392 expedition from Kings Lynn

We can date the formal start of the Lynn crusade from the reappointment on 15th June 1392 of Richard de Kyngston as Henry of Derby's Treasurer for War. This was followed by letters of protection issued on 27th June 1392 by King Richard II in favour of his cousin Henry of Derby and his companions Hugh and Richard Waterton. Letters of protection protected their property from any legal action while they were away. Crusading was an expensive activity, and the accounts record Henry's father, John Duke of Lancaster, granting payments to his son 'for his voyage to Prussia'.

Unlike the 1390 expedition which started from Boston, the 1392 campaign assembled at Lynn on the opposite side of the Wash. We do not know why Lynn was chosen in preference to Boston — most likely practical logistics determined the location. However, it is worth noting that Lynn was a centre of the cult of St Margaret of Antioch, a popular saint amongst crusaders and especially venerated by the Teutonic knights (see *The saintly ladies of the Teutonic knights*, April 19, 2016 The University of Birmingham Centre for the Study of the Middle Ages).

Did Henry wish to celebrate the Feast of St Margaret on 20th July 1392 before he set sail on the crusade? Coincidentally the 1390 crusade left Boston on 20th July, mentioned in the accounts as 'St Margaret's Day'. Did Henry regard St Margaret of Antioch as a protector of his crusading force and the period around the 20th July as an auspicious period to set off?

Three ships were fitted out in Lynn including cabins for the senior knights of the expedition. Spices were purchased from London and

sent to Lynn for the voyage. Henry's retainers assembled in the town and four boats of Henry's baggage arrived from Peterborough.

Ten boats were hired to tow the ships from Lynn to Heacham, a prosperous port a few miles along the coast from Lynn, part of the very wealthy maritime Wash economy (the *Inquisitio Navium* of 1337 mentions 12 Heacham tenants who owned

St Margaret's minster in Kings Lynn, with the fishing ships). On Tuesday
Saturday market place in the foreground. 24th July 1392 the expedition set sail from Heacham. The journey took just over two weeks across the North Sea and around Denmark, and the ships arrived in Danzig on 10th August 1392.

Henry stayed in Danzig for two weeks. Danzig was a major Hanseatic port, dominated by its Krantor — a massive crane gate that symbolised the city's commercial dominance of the Baltic. There was a significant English community living in Danzig at this time (some 40 years later the mystic Margery Kempe travelled from Lynn to Danzig, illustrating the comparative ease of travel between the two centres).

On 25th August the expedition set off for Elbing (Elblag) staying at the abbey for two days as a guest of the Augustinians (the accounts record Henry making offerings to the abbey on the 29th August).

On 31st August the army reached Braunsberg (Braniewo). Originally settled by citizens of Lübeck it had a formidable hill-top stone castle where Henry would have stayed. The battle flag of this town can be seen in the 1415 *Banderia Prutenorum* manuscript and was divided into two parts — a black cross on a white background above a white cross on a black background.

Moving on, Henry arrived at Königsberg on 2nd September. Here he was received with great courtly ceremony. Henry's army would have been a dazzling sight, a display of martial might designed in every way to impress. One can surmise the sense of anticipation that accompanied the marshalling of the troops in this great Hanseatic city. Assembled in chivalric glory, heraldic majesty and knightly magnificence, the English force was poised to advance. But...

...the crusade just fizzled out. There seems to have been an abrupt change of plans. The accounts tell us Henry was back in Danzig on 7th September.

What happened?

John Capgrave (the Lynn chronicler) says 'the lords of the province were not friendly to his desire.' In other words the Grand Master of the Teutonic Knights did not want Henry around. He had been asked to leave.

It must have been a humiliating moment for Henry and his small army. It would be like the England Football Team today qualifying for a World Cup, only to be kicked out in the opening round. The loss of prestige must have been mortifying.

We know that the Order paid Henry £400 (a huge sum, perhaps £10 million in today's money) as compensation for his efforts. The Marshal of the Teutonic Knights, Engelhardt Rabe, met Henry at Königsberg, perhaps to smooth things over. This indicates the Teutonic Order were embarrassed by what had happened.

There are three theories about why Henry was asked to leave:

- Theory 1: The Annals of Thorn say that there was a dispute over the right to carry the banner of St George — a saint honoured by both England and the Teutonic Knights.
- Theory 2: While in Danzig some of Henry's men killed a man called 'Hans' and his servant and this led to bad feeling and

unrest in the city. Hans and his servant were buried at Henry's expense and oblations were paid for and alms given to the poor, which indicates Henry admitting responsibility for the deaths. The nineteenth-century German Professor Hans Prutz has said these funeral ceremonies were held in the Marienkirche, the vast brick church in the centre of Danzig (Gdansk).

- Theory 3: Historian Chris Given-Wilson in his *Henry IV* (2016) argues that the Lithuanian civil war was coming to an end, and no longer welcomed military intervention from outsiders.

Whatever the reason, Henry and his entourage were now faced with the question: what do we do now?

They obtained safe conduct from the Duke of Stolpe to travel through Pomerania, and left Danzig on 22nd September and went to Schonee where they stayed for two days. Valets were sent on ahead to make preparations and arrange supplies. From Schonee the army progressed to Hammerstein, Poleschken, Schievelbein, Dramberg, Arneswald, Landsberg, and Drossen, arriving at Frankfurt on Oder on 4th October 1392.

By 13th October they had arrived in Prague where they stayed with King Wenceslas (brother of Queen Anne of Bohemia, wife of Henry's cousin Richard II). They stayed at the royal court in Prague for 11 days. This sojourn must have gone a long way to restoring Henry's injured pride and confirming his status as a great prince, honoured and welcomed throughout Europe.

During his time in Prague Henry made devotional visits to Hradschin Castle, and also gave offerings at the relics in Karlstein Castle (this high Gothic castle had been founded in 1348 by Holy Roman Emperor Charles IV as a place of safekeeping for royal treasures, especially Charles's collection of holy relics).

On 4th November the army arrived in Vienna. At some point between leaving Danzig and arriving in Vienna Henry seems to have developed the idea of transmuting his crusade to the Baltic into a pilgrimage to Jerusalem. On a practical level, Henry was replacing one high-status expedition with another, thus avoiding any suggestion that he had been dishonoured by the events in Königsberg. However, the change of destination is also interesting in terms of crusading ideology, reinforcing the pilgrimage aspect of the Baltic crusades. It is easy to be beguiled by the descriptions of lavish feasting and jousting and to see the Baltic crusades as sybaritic experiences, indulgent and hedonistic. And yet during the course of both crusades we see Henry visiting shrines, venerating relics, giving alms to religious institutions.

With help of Albert Duke of Austria Henry sent letters to Venice, arranging for a ship to take him to the Holy Land. This ship was a hull and needed to be fitted up, armed and provisioned. Therefore Henry travelled to Venice in a leisurely way, allowing time to prepare the ship and buy provisions.

Henry stayed outside Venice over the winter months, lodging at the nearby town of Portogruaro. Parts of this town have not changed in the intervening centuries and so visitors today will see the town hall and abbey much as the English crusaders/pilgrims did. During this period stores were purchased, visits to shrines were made.

Henry went into Venice for 21 days. Capgrave's chronicle records that during this time he was received by the Doge Antonio Venier who lived in magnificent style as ruler of the city state. Venice was the principal port of departure for the Holy Land at this period; and from 1291 to 1309 Venice had been the headquarters of the Teutonic Knights.

Purchases of food and drink for the voyage to Jerusalem were huge and included: salted oxen; 2,250 eggs, plus live poultry; barrels of water, cheese, oil, potted ducks, fish, vegetables, condiments and spices; 2,000 dates; 1,000 pounds of almonds; wines in amphora and barrels; 40 sacks of biscuits and bread; and four barrels of fruit.

A coin depicting Doge Antonio Venier.

About 50 men accompanied Henry on the voyage to Jerusalem, the rest remaining at Portogruaro. Amongst those selected were Granson, Erpingham, Willoughby, Mowbray the herald, Henry the Henchman, Bucton the Steward, and Kyngston the Treasurer. We also see mentioned John de Radington (or Ridlington), Lord Prior of the Order of St John of Jerusalem in England (the crusading order of Knights Hospitallers), whom Henry seems to have met whilst in Venice.

The expedition sailed on 22nd or 23rd December 1392. On Christmas Day they attended a service at Zara (now Zadar) on the Dalmatian coast. After rounding the Peloponnese peninsula Henry's ship headed for the island of Rhodes.

Henry made a short stay at Rhodes, which at this time was the headquarters of the Knights of St John of Jerusalem (the Knights Hospitallers). Henry visited the Grand Master of the Order, taking Prior de Radington with him. The Knights Hospitallers lived in great chivalric style, and the encounter between the Grand Master and the English prince would have been a significant occasion.

It is worth noting at this point that the accounts show Henry's table linen being washed and laundered many times which indicates the English party enjoyed formal dining, and were concerned about hygiene.

Leaving Rhodes the English party crossed the Mediterranean and arrived in Jaffa in the Holy Land. They found a ruined city as Jaffa had been conquered by the Egyptian Mamluks led by Baibars and completely destroyed in 1268. Following the Muslim reconquest of the Holy Land the new overlords gave western pilgrims safe passage to the Christian holy places.

There is no mention in the accounts relating to the hire of horse, so Henry and his companions probably walked from Jaffa to Jerusalem, a distance of 40 miles. They spent ten days in Jerusalem and would have visited the Holy Sepulchre and the major shrines, churches and monasteries. The accounts do not mention much apart from the buying of candles which indicates a serious and devout mood to the sojourn in Jerusalem.

Returning by foot to Jaffa, they sailed to Famagusta in Cyprus where they were received by King James I. Cyprus had been a crusader kingdom for nearly two hundred years. The capital, Famagusta, was dominated by the magnificent fourteenth-century cathedral of St Nicholas. During his stay in Cyprus Henry acquired a leopard – which required its own cabin on the ship. He was also presented with falcons and a parrot. A converted 'Sarasin' joined the party at this point.

From Cyprus Henry sailed back to Venice, arriving there on 20th March 1393. He travelled overland to Paris, and the accounts record him as giving alms to a madman at Amiens. On 28th June he arrived at

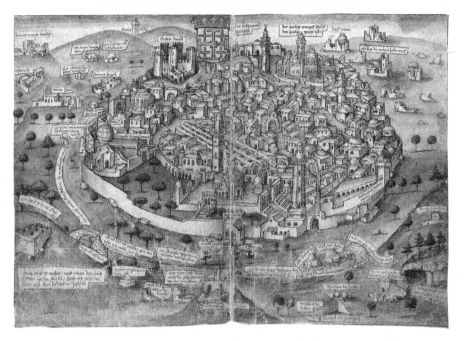

A medieval depiction of Jerusalem from Conrad Grünenberg's 'Description of the journey from Constance to Jerusalem'.

Calais (which was English territory) and by 5th July 1393 he was back in London.

One can imagine the sense of triumph which accompanied his homecoming. The prestige locally, nationally and internationally would have been tremendous. Not only had Henry proved himself as a leader, a warrior and a loyal defender of the Holy Church, he had announced in the clearest possible way his suitability as a potential king.

It was a message that would not go unnoticed in the court of his cousin, King Richard II. The kudos gained from knightly exploits such as these two crusades gave Henry the chivalric aura that identified him as a potential warrior-king. Henry was later able to channel this emotional endorsement into a practical movement that eventually enabled him to challenge his cousin Richard and establish himself as King Henry IV, first ruler of the House of Lancaster.

Lynn and the German Hanse in the 14th & 15th centuries: Danzig

Paul Richards

An Essay based on a lecture delivered at the History and Archaeology Symposium in King's Lynn on 21st May 2016.

I

English historians have normally used the label 'Hanseatic League' to describe those 70 or more large north German towns whose impact on European economic development was marked between 1250 and 1550. A notable exception is T.H. Lloyd's *England and the German Hanse 1157–1618* (1991). Continental scholars have increasingly identified the Hanse as a far more informal urban confederation with economic goals distinct from a league which implies a formal political organisation. The question of what the Hanse actually was or was not does not concern this essay. Suffice to stress that it sprang from hanses or associations of German merchants seeking to secure trading rights across Europe. It is not until the 1350s that the Hanse seems suddenly to become 'the towns of the German Hanse' in response to the attempts by the authorities in Bruges and Flanders to curb German commercial liberties. Hence the meeting at Lübeck in 1358 which is recognised as the first Congress or Hansetag of the German towns. Unlike a league, however, there was no founding charter or official launch, though Bremen asked Cologne to search the archives for one in 1418!

Despite the fact that the majority of Hanseatic towns had little or nothing to do with England, the most important ones did, Lübeck, Hamburg, Bremen, Stralsund, Cologne and Danzig especially. London and England's east coast ports were major trading partners of these German cities, with Lynn, Boston, Hull, Colchester, Yarmouth and Ipswich all noteworthy. Hanseatic merchants were the most successful of the alien communities trading in late medieval England accounting for at least 15 percent of its foreign trade. They acquired exceptional commercial privileges arising from royal charters endorsed by successive Kings who believed the Germans contributed greatly to the nation's wealth. To establish the place and significance of Lynn in Hanseatic Europe before 1550 is the principal aim of a forthcoming book. The focus of this essay is Lynn's connection to Prussia and to Danzig in particular. Its merchants were in the vanguard of English trading ventures into the eastern Baltic from the 1380s. Though Lynn's commercial links with the Low Countries and France were also well established, the town's economy became most dependent on the Baltic and Norway.

The medieval names of Hanseatic towns are used throughout the essay, but it should be noted that Danzig is now Gdańsk in Poland. I prefer Lynn (as in local parlance) to King's Lynn and the town was anyway 'Bishop's Lynn' until 1537. To Lindsey Bavin I would like to record my appreciation for her assistance in the preparation of this essay.

II

A key aspect of the emergence of the German Hanse as the major force in northern European economic development is colonisation from the West of Slavonic enclaves or territories to the east of Lübeck, partly as a result of continental population growth in the 13th century. The six Prussian towns belonging to the confederation by the late 14th century were Danzig (Gdańsk), Elbing (Eblag), Königsberg (Kaliningrad), Braunsberg (Braniewo), Kulm (Chemno), and Thorn (Toruń). Its extensive hinterland embraced by the Vistula river system ensured Danzig became Prussia's premier port by the 1380s. Wax, fish, iron, copper, timber and amber went from its harbour to Lübeck with salt and cloth going in the opposite direction (a ship took four days and a waggon two weeks). Danzig also included Königberg, Riga, Reval (Tallinn), Stockholm and Visby on Gotland amongst its principal trading partners.

Danzig and the Prussian towns were not self-governing centres which could independently join urban organisations. Though members of the German Hanse in their own right, these towns were under the suzerainty of the Grand Master of the Teutonic Order, the sole territorial prince admitted to it. Wars with Poland and Lithuania eventually resulted in the Treaty of Thorn (1466) whereby the Teutonic Knights surrendered Danzig and West Prussia to the Polish Crown.

The Teutonic Knights gave Prussia internal security and played a key role in the growth of Danzig, Stettin, Thorn, Elbing and Königsberg as well as owning landed estates from which timber and cereals were marketed through Hanseatic trading networks. Danzig took an active part in Hanseatic Congresses from 1361 and in the meetings of the Prussian towns where its leadership is indicated by the claim that 'it had to pay the greater part of the cost of all the diplomatic and military undertakings of the Hanseatic League' [Biernat & Cieslak: 48]. Funds were raised by the pound tax imposed on shipping through Danzig for the military operations of the German Hanse such as the successful war against Denmark in the 1360s.

From the later 14th century Danzig became the head Hanseatic seaport in the eastern Baltic supplying timber and forest products to western Europe. Its big ships sailed around Denmark into the North Sea. Such long distance carriage of low value bulk cargoes might be possible several times a year for vessels whose destination was Lynn or Boston, though the weather from November to February usually prohibited voyages. Danzig's vast hinterland served by the river Vistula guaranteed the success of the port. Tar, pitch, flax, hemp and timber from the Baltic lands were much in demand from ship builders in western Europe. Cereals were regularly exported from Danzig to England and Flanders, particularly when there was a poor harvest in the West. Iron from Sweden with some copper and lead from Central Europe were also carried as ballast by Prussian ships sailing to Bruges and London. English merchants found buoyant new markets for cloth in Prussia and eastern Europe.

Stuart Jenks emphasises how the character of the Hanseatic

presence in Lynn changed after 1353 when the port was excluded from the English staple towns (towns appointed by the King to export wool and other commodities to facilitate tax collection). Germans dealing in wool and stockfish, particularly from Lübeck, decamped to Boston. When Lynn became a staple port in 1373 and a separate customs district again, no longer lumped with Boston by the royal officials, Prussians had replaced Lübeckers. Before 1353 the ships of Lübeck and the Wendish towns were more common in Lynn than those from Danzig and the eastern Baltic, but the latter now began to appear in greater numbers, in the Humber as well as the Great Ouse. The Norfolk port was now trading more with the eastern rather than the western Baltic using both German vessels and its own fleet, reflecting the rise of its merchant class. Shipping between Lynn and other North Sea havens such as Hamburg, Bremen and Kampen remained important, but Baltic commerce was more lucrative.

The late 14th century is a watershed in England's economic history which was to impact profoundly on Anglo-Hanseatic commercial relations. Though raw wool exports continued to be fairly buoyant into the 1440s, the outflow of cloth increased as the national textile industry developed apace. More wool was being used at home. Running parallel

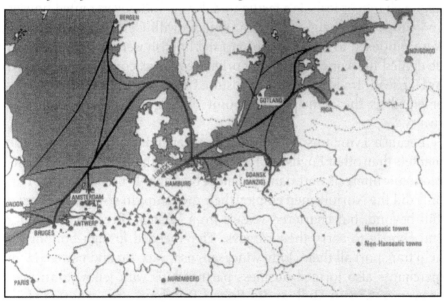

The trade routes of the Hanseatic League around 1400.

to the expansion of England's cloth industry, and clearly a direct consequence of it, its merchants were now venturing into the eastern Baltic with cargoes of cloth to exchange for forest products. Lynn and Hull men were prominent because they imported more timber in exchange for cloth than the other English east coast ports, including London. Then the English began to claim similar trading rights in Baltic seaports as exercised by the Germans in Lynn or Boston. This issue of reciprocity aggravated a series of Anglo-Hanseatic disputes in the course of the 15th century.

<h1 style="text-align:center">III</h1>

Danzigers had become the most numerous Hanseatic traders in Lynn by the 1370s and 1380s demonstrating that the commercial interests of the Wash port were moving eastwards. Its merchants had in turn established footholds in Prussian seaports, alongside men from Boston, Hull and other English east coast havens. Robert Borkesham (died 1411) imported timber and pitch from the Baltic and mainly exported cloth to Danzig and Bremen as well as Dordrecht for example. English merchants not only exported cloth but distributed it in Danzig and its region, thus arousing local resentment. They appeared to be taking charge of Prussia's textile trade! And, moreover, rented houses and shops in Danzig rather than lodging with German hosts as they were supposed to do. For their part the English were very unhappy to be denied the same commercial privileges or tax concessions enjoyed by Hanseatic traders in Lynn or Boston. Unsurprisingly, Prussia rapidly emerged as the principal flashpoint of Anglo-Hanseatic economic rivalry.

Because Lynn was becoming more dependent on eastern Baltic markets than other English ports, perhaps with the exception of Hull, its economic interests were damaged more by Anglo-Prussian conflict. Not only did the Norfolk men employ their own ships in voyages to Danzig and beyond, but chartered vessels from Wismar, Bremen, Hamburg and Danzig to carry their cargoes. They needed foreign bottoms to help transport all their cloth, wine, salt, fish, wax, tin and pewter. Lynn merchants also formed business partnerships with fellow townsmen or even traders in Hull, as did Robert Brunham, who exported cloth and corn from the 1390s. But the periodic arrest of English ships and confiscation of their cargoes in the Baltic undermined Lynn's overseas commerce. Lists of English losses in trade with Prussia (1370—88 and 1388—1436 and 1474—1491) demonstrate that its merchants accounted for at least one third of all damages claimed. During their early years in the eastern Baltic, the Englanders catalogued numerous complaints about Prussian embezzlement, extortion, robbery and arrest of their ships as well as piracy. All this confirms how much Lynn's commerce was pressing 'inexorably eastwards' as Jenks emphasises [Friedland & Richards: 100].

Trouble for English merchants in Prussia could spring from events in far away west Europe. In May 1385 an English royal fleet had attacked and robbed six Prussian ships in the estuary of the Zwin, not far from Bruges, because the Germans were allegedly supporting the King's Flemish enemy. In July 1385 a meeting of Prussian towns reacted by ordering the seizure of English merchandise in Danzig and Elbing and banned all trade with England. The English Parliament in October 1385 retaliated by ordering the arrest of all Prussian property from London north to the Wash ports, where most was likely to be located, and by June 1386 enough had been found to cover English losses in Prussia.

To take direct action against merchants and their ships to satisfy grievances of whatever kind was not only testimony to the failure of Anglo-Prussian diplomacy; it stopped trade, destroyed businesses and sometimes cost lives. Peace was in the interests of both sides. In April 1386 a Prussian embassy had arrived in London to talk to the King's Council but no compromise was possible on the Zwin incident. Then Richard II decided to send an embassy to Prussia to negotiate a general Anglo-Prussian settlement with the Grand Master of the Teutonic Order. Representatives from Lynn, London, Colchester, Ipswich, Yarmouth, Norwich, Boston and Hull were called to London in the summer of 1386 to provide information on commercial losses in Prussia. It was clearly essential that the royal ambassadors to the Grand Master Conrad Rotherstein at Marienburg were as fully briefed as possible. Lynn was at the forefront of these preparations. Its merchants had submitted a claim for damages of nearly £2000 following English arrests in Prussia in 1385 which was 'the largest of any town' despite being reduced by half [Lloyd: 91]. No less than ten royal letters were sent to Lynn in 1388 in connection with the Anglo-Prussian dispute.

Two ambassadors to Prussian were appointed: Walter Sibille of London and Thomas Graa of York were merchants, assisted by a royal clerk called Nicholas Stocket. They were joined by John Bebys or Bevys of London who was to act as their 'informer' [Lloyd: 65]. In June 1388 they set sail for Prussia from Lynn on a ship requisitioned into the King's service. The considerable cost of the embassy was met from the funds accumulated in Lynn from its recent arrest of Prussian vessels following the King's writ in retaliation for attacks on English ships in Prussia. John Brunham, thrice mayor of the town and alderman of the Holy Trinity Guild, had been commissioned by the King's Council to transfer these funds from Lynn to London, and duly delivered £340 to the mayor of the capital. The King prohibited English cloth and other exports to Prussia whilst his embassy was on its mission. Lynn, York, Yarmouth, Newcastle, Hull, Boston, Colchester, Ipswich, Sandwich, Southampton and Bristol were the ports mainly affected by the ban. From the first the King's Council had made it clear to the merchants from these towns that they would eventually have to pay for the embassy to Prussia. They would be individually assessed on their goods and valuables released by the Prussians once an Anglo-Prussian agreement had been signed.

The English embassy presented its credentials to the Grand Master of the Teutonic Order at Marienburg on 28 July 1388 and began negotiations with his representatives who consulted the Prussian towns. The Anglo-Prussian Treaty of Marienburg was sealed on 21 August 1388. The urgent need for Prussian and English merchants to secure satisfactory outcomes to the claims for damages in the courts of their host nations was recognised. Hanseatic privileges in England were reaffirmed by the English whose freedom to live and trade in Prussia was likewise endorsed by the Germans. The treaty was too general and unspecific to give the English the same commercial concessions enjoyed by the Hanseatic towns abroad. There was to be no kontor in Danzig on a par with that in London! Nevertheless, the King's ambassadors had concluded an important international treaty with Conrad Rothenstein, the Grand Master at Marienburg, and England's position in Prussia seemed more secure as a result.

What happened after the signing of the Treaty of Marienburg in 1388? Steps were immediately taken by Richard II to ensure that

Prussian merchants whose ships and goods had been arrested in England had their possessions and money returned. The mayors of London and other towns trading with Prussia had been the custodians of such property. The King reminded his subjects in October 1388 that peaceful commercial operations between England and Prussia required both sides to enact the provisions of the treaty. Moreover, all the English towns with trading connections to Prussia were ordered to send at least one representative to London, there to establish exactly what must be done 'for ending the matter'. York, Beverley, Norwich, Boston, Hull and Colchester were also told to recompense Lynn for bearing the costs of the recent embassy to the East. They were obliged to send an official to Lynn to pay John Brunham the amounts for which their merchants had been assessed in proportion to their claims against the Prussians. About 20 Lynn merchants were also assessed to help fund the King's embassy to Prussia. Roger Paxman, John Atte Lathe, Walter Urry, Thomas Waterden, Henry Betele, John Kempe, John Brandon, John Loke and others read like a roll call of the town's 'potentiores'. Paxman was mayor in 1388 and assessed for more than any of his colleagues. Beverley men had still failed to pay their share in April 1389 and faced the King's 'wrath' and large fines as a consequence. In November 1389 Lynn's mayor had still not returned to Prussian merchants in the town all their confiscated property. He appears to have been jogged into action by the King's Council fearful no doubt that 'no new dispute arise' between England and Prussia [Harrison: 143]. Prussian goods must have been kept in the undercroft of the Holy Trinity Guildhall on the Saturday Market Place or in warehouses belonging to the town.

In the summer of 1389 following the Treaty of Marienburg a Prussian delegation travelled to London to monitor English compliance with the agreement. One of the German ambassadors visited Lynn, 100 miles north of the capital, to consult with its authorities whose special interest in the Baltic was well known. He received gifts of wine and even oats for his horses. However, this Prussian lord returned to London shortly before the dinner in his honour at the Trinity Guildhall, hence leaving Mayor Paxman and Bishop Spenser waiting. Expenses relating to the diplomatic visit were not inconsiderable, including the time of the Norwich bishop's cook and other servants, though the guests no doubt soon consumed the fine repast!

The Kieler Hansekogge is a replica of a ship built in Bremen in 1380 and rebuilt in Kiel in 1989. Such vessels sailed between the Wash ports and the Baltic.

IV

Lynn was in the forefront of England's commercial expansion eastwards and 'staking its prosperity' on trade with the Baltic and Norway [Lloyd: 91]. Between April and September 1390 at least 43 of its own ships entered the Wash port with cargoes from abroad, of which 26 came from the Baltic and two from Norway. Some merchants took their families from England's east coast ports to Danzig and other Prussian towns where they rented houses and warehouses. Single men sometimes married German women. All this did not directly affect Lübeck and the Hanseatic towns in the western Baltic, but it encouraged Prussian resentment. Then Lynn men were almost certainly prominent in the English Company established in Danzig by 1404 and endorsed by Henry IV. It had its own constitution or ordinances with the maintenance of good business practice and social discipline priorities. Prussians fears that the English planned to found a trading post on a par with those German *kontors* in London or Bergen were revived.

Anglo-Prussian relations became fragile once again in the first decade of the 15th century. Though a Hanseatic Congress at Lübeck in

1405 had shown solidarity with Prussia in its quest to extract damages for commercial losses at the hands of the English, even declaring a halt to the export and import trades with England, the ban could not be enforced because other Hanseatic towns disagreed. London was an important market for the wine and industrial goods of Cologne and the Rhineland towns which wanted English cloth; nor did all Prussians wish to cut profitable economic ties with England. Prussia's overlord, the Grand Master of the Teutonic Order sitting in his Marienburg fortress, had moreover political reasons to curry favour with the islanders in the West. Pagan tribes on his eastern border were in a state of unrest and the kingdom of Poland was asserting its power in eastern Europe. Henry IV was himself a member of the Order of Teutonic Knights and saw an opportunity to conclude a treaty with Prussia alone; Lübeck would be excluded and the German Hanse divided.

Diplomatic exchanges between England and Prussia in 1403 and 1404 had failed to restore harmony between the two countries, but progress was possible by 1407, and Lynn played its accustomed leading role in peace talks. The town's big investment in trade with the Baltic cities made its merchants the experts in this branch of English foreign affairs as Jenks observes:

> 'Every single English embassy which negotiated with the Hanse
> in the 15th century included a Lynn merchant. Indeed, in 1408,
> Henry IV ordered Lynn to send a delegation post haste to the
> council in London, since Prussian delegates had arrived and,
> as the King said, 'The men of Lynn understand commerce
> in Prussia better than any other merchants of the realm'
> [Friedland & Richards: 101].

A Lynn merchant called John Brown looms large as a representative of his town in English embassies abroad and meetings with Prussian politicians at home. In 1405 Brown took Henry IV's letter to Prussia granting his merchants in eastern and northern Europe the power to elect a governor and he may have already been 'nominated' as that man [Lloyd: 115]. He played a part in the making of the Anglo-Prussian treaty of 1410 which Hanseatic towns outside Prussia saw as conceding too much to the English, but it did little more in reality than bring an end to hostilities. Henry IV had agreed to guarantee payments of damages to Prussian merchants who had been demanding compensation for losses blamed on the English since the 1380s. Anglo-Hanseatic disputes in the 1430s led to yet another peace settlement called the Treaty of London (1437) which the English again interpreted in a more favourable light than the Germans.

V

What kind of town was Danzig in the early 15th century? It was an expanding Baltic port of approximately 15000 inhabitants which had long attracted migrants from western Europe. Danzig was also a manufacturing centre with many artisans but 'the merchants were the group of people who brought most glory to Gdansk and made it famous internationally' whilst 'acquiring the greatest influence in the city' [Biernat & Cieslak:47]. The English appear to have settled in a district known as 'Long Garden'. They gathered with other aliens at the *Artushof* or Merchants' Exchange, built in the 14th century, though the present facade of 'Arthur's Court' dates from 1617. Urban markets and fairs were eagerly frequented by foreigners in Prussia too. Before 1300 an annual fair began on the feast of St Dominic (5th August) when merchants could engage in free trading, as well as finding entertainment. English, Dutch, Spanish and French traders mingled with Russians and Germans to stock up for autumn shipments to the West. Danzig could, however, be a turbulent city. In 1363 conflict between Germans and Poles had erupted at the Dominican Fair, with the latter targeting the Teutonic Knights in their rallying cry, but the Poles were 'beaten and many perished' [Biernat & Cieslak: 64]. At this time the Poles numbered not more than 10 per cent of Danzig's inhabitants, though its Slavonic population increased in the 15th century through migration from the countryside.

It seems not an inconsiderable number of English people were passengers on merchant ships sailing to and from the Baltic by 1400; sailors, apprentices, servants and family members were temporary residents in Danzig and other northern and eastern German towns. Did some settle permanently? A valuable insight into Anglo-Prussian connections in the 15th century comes from 'The Book of Margery Kempe' believed to be the first autobiography of an English person.

Margery (c.1373–1441) was the daughter of John Brunham who was chief amongst the merchant rulers of later 14th century Lynn. She married another less noteworthy merchant called John Kempe. Margery's amazing life story as a religious mystic and pilgrim can be found in her book. One of her sons was an overseas trader who had earlier lapsed into a promiscuous life style before finding love and marriage with a German woman in Danzig. In 2015 Professor Sobecki of Groningen University found a letter in a Gdańsk archive which appears to substantiate Margery's account of her son's adventures.

Danzig as it appeared circa 1628.

Lynn sailors arriving in Danzig around 1400 would have been impressed with its great crane, slightly leaning over the Motlawa river. It is first mentioned in 1367. The structure burnt down in 1442 before being rebuilt in 1443, partly in brick, to the design seen today. It was restored after severe damage in the Second World War. The great crane was used to erect masts on ships as well as for loading and unloading vessels, with the power coming from men walking inside the two huge wooden wheels. It also served a defence function for the medieval city as one of its gates on the harbour. Danzig was a major shipbuilding centre and new methods allowed bigger vessels to be constructed. In 1412 a Hanseatic Congress decreed against the building of ships too large to access some of the more shallow Baltic harbours. Both Dutch and English purchased ships in Danzig and sometimes shared ownership of vessels with German merchants, but Hanseatic towns became increasingly opposed to both practices, fearing further foreign competition.

VI

Anglo-German relations became strained in 1447 when Henry VI issued an ultimatum to the Hanseatic towns that their privileges in England would be abolished unless English merchants in the Baltic had similar benefits. Talks were held in Lübeck to reach an agreement but no progress was possible. Then hopes for an Anglo-Hanseatic settlement were dashed in May 1449 when English privateers captured a great fleet of 110 Hanseatic and Netherlandish vessels in the Channel. It had been sailing north from near Nantes in France transporting wine and salt back to the Baltic; 16 Lübeck and 14 Danzig ships were in the convoy. The latter and other German vessels were robbed of their cargoes after being taken to the Isle of Wight. Robert Wenington had led this bold but stupid act of international piracy which sacrificed the national interest to private greed. How far he had been encouraged to attack the Hanseatic fleet by London politicians around the King is uncertain but it was a 'pivotal incident' in Anglo-Hanseatic relations which worsened 'and remained a source of bitter enmity for two decades' [Fudge:18].

The seizure of the Hanseatic ships in 1449 seemed certain to have serious repercussions for Boston and Lynn whose overseas trade largely depended on Lübeck and Danzig respectively. Yet Danzig resisted Lübeck's insistence that retaliation should be immediate unless compensation was swiftly paid, clearly because its merchants profited more from Anglo-German commerce. English merchants in Prussia had been arrested and their goods confiscated, though an Anglo-Hanseatic meeting in Bruges in November 1449 avoided a war. Baltic naval stores were too important for England to lose.

Slow progress in mending Anglo-Hanseatic relations after the adverse impact on trade caused by the attack on the Bay fleet in 1449 was undone in 1458. England's so-called 'King Maker' and governor of Calais, the Earl of Warwick, instigated an assault by English privateers on another Hanseatic Bay fleet transporting salt from La Rochelle to the Baltic. No fewer than 18 Lübeck ships were seized. Once again the Lübeckers did not win the enthusiastic support they expected from the

other Hanseatic towns for counter attacks on English vessels in the
Baltic. Danzig, less hurt by losses than Lübeck as a result of Warwick's
plunder of the Bay fleet, warned English merchants to venture into the
Baltic only in convoys, though seven Lynn merchants were temporarily
imprisoned there. Trade between England's east coast ports and the
Baltic was now confined to Danzig, but by the 1460s there were signs
of a trade revival, despite one English ship homeward bound to the
Wash port being taken by Lübeckers. Hanseatic ships from Danzig
were arriving in Lynn and Hull with Baltic goods for return cargoes of
cloth. Some Prussian vessels unloaded timber and forest products in
England before sailing to the Bay of Biscay for salt which was carried
to the Baltic. A certain Hilderbrand van der Wald of Danzig imported
Baltic goods at Lynn in November 1459, departed for France (probably
in ballast), then appeared in his home port in 1460 'laden with salt'
[Fudge:42].

Trade between the Wash ports and Prussia had been ongoing since
1449, even if in modest amounts, but the situation changed in 1454.
Danzig seceded from Prussia and placed itself under the suzerainty of
the Polish King who granted the city exclusive control over its shipping
and commerce in 1457. Though the Danzigers wanted Anglo-Hanseatic
trade to flourish, in contrast to Lübeck's hostility towards England, they
curbed the commercial freedom the English had exploited under the
Grand Master of the Teutonic Order. Lynn merchants were particularly
affected. Jenks underlines the impact of Danzig's new economic policy
on the Wash port:

> While this did not affect the volume of trade with Lynn, it
> did shift its terms. Although Danzig was more than willing to
> grant Lynn shippers and merchants safe conducts for trade, it
> was now free to deny any Englishmen the right of abode, and
> this destroyed the English cloth distribution system, which
> depended on resident factors. As a result, Prussian merchants
> for the first time in the 15th century consistently handled over
> half the traffic with Lynn [Friedland & Richards:102].

Nevertheless, English traders were still resident in Danzig, including
Lynn men like John Thoresby who bought a ship there in 1457. In 1454

Hull and Lynn were given safe conduct to Danzig where their merchants exchanged cloth, grain, pewter and hides for the usual Baltic goods. But Danzig ships carried most of the timber and forest products (wax and pitch especially) unloaded at Lynn and Hull.

Commercial intercourse between Danzig and Lynn was regular if unimpressive in the 1460s. German merchants could expect a cogge to complete the voyage two or three times in a calendar year as Fudge shows. The Danzig trader, Paul Roole, moored in the Ouse in December 1467 and sailed for his home port with cloth at the end of February 1468; he was back in the Wash port unloading wood, iron and canvas in May. At Whitsuntide 1468 he was entering the Baltic on the return voyage to the East, but appears again in Lynn in August with a cargo of boards, oars, tar and iron. Thus Roole had completed two return journeys between Lynn and Danzig in about five months. He seems not to have strictly followed the decree issued by a Hanseatic Congress in 1403 that navigation was to be prohibited between 11th November and 22nd February each year because of snow and ice. Baltic seaborne trade more or less ceased during the winter as a result, though the ban was applied less rigorously in the North Sea. This must have reduced the number of ship wrecks but curtailed Hanseatic commerce because vessels could be laid up in North European ports for three months of every year. It should be noted that foreign ships were usually banned from wintering in Hanseatic ports whose authorities were no doubt reluctant to offer shelter to their competitors!

Lynn merchants were exporting more cloth in the 1450s and 1460s than Hanseatic merchants who were responsible for about a quarter of the total leaving the Wash harbour. But cloth exports from English east coast havens were considerably lower in these decades than in the 1440s as London began to dominate the trade. Easterlings sailed to Lynn and Hull not so much to buy cloth as to sell Baltic goods for distribution in their hinterlands via the Great Ouse and Humber river systems respectively. Lloyd assesses the quantity and character of Anglo-Hanseatic trade through the Norfolk port thus:

> Although comparatively small, the Hanse trade at Lynn in the
> 1460s was clearly well established and engaged the interest
> of the same ships and merchants year after year, some ships

coming two or three times each year. It was essentially an Anglo-Baltic trade, chiefly occupying Danzig and Hamburg ships, and some of it probably followed the Hamburg-Lübeck route. Amongst the merchants involved can be identified men from Hamburg, Danzig and Cologne, though it is impossible to establish the exact proportions of each [Lloyd:227].

VII

In June 1468 a small fleet of 10 English merchant ships circumnavigated Jutland on its voyage to the eastern Baltic, but seven were arrested by the Danes and two were from Lynn. The Danish King was also the overlord of Iceland where he said the English, and Lynn men in particular, had committed heinous crimes. This relatively minor international incident sparked a Sea War (1469–73) in the southern North Sea between England and the Hanseatic towns. Hotheads around Edward IV blamed the German Hanse for instigating the Danish action against the English fleet. Peace was secured at Utrecht in 1474 when the English King confirmed German ownership of *kontors* at London and Boston but also granted them a new trading post at Lynn.

Though Lübeck called upon Danzig to take responsibility for the Lynn *kontor* because its merchants frequented the Wash port more than those of any other Hanseatic city, the Prussians did not ratify the Treaty of Utrecht until 1476. In the interim the Danzigers must have made arrangements for their English friends in the town to manage it. Henry Baxter, Henry Patenmaker and Thomas Wright were the trio in question 'who had stuck to them loyally since the dark days of 1468' [Friedland & Richards:103]. Wright had already been instrumental in the process which resulted in the King conveying these Lynn premises to the German *kontor* in London in April 1475. Jenks concludes that Lynn's merchant rulers 'wanted' the German Hanse and in particular their former trading partners from Danzig 'to re-establish a presence in Lynn' [Friedland & Richards: 106].

The Anglo-Hanseatic Sea War (1469–73) brought trade between Danzig and Lynn to a halt, but Easterlings sailed back into the Norfolk harbour in late 1474, no doubt testimony to the close ties between German and English merchants. Hull was also being revisited by

Hanseatic ships, though its merchants were now drawn more to the Low Countries than the Baltic. Anglo-Hanseatic commerce at Boston and Ipswich did not recover to any degree. Participation by English east coast ports in the Baltic trade became concentrated in the hands of Lynn men who used both English and German vessels to reconnect with Danzig. The Prussian city was becoming one of Europe's great seaports linking East and West. In 1474 there were 403 and in 1490 no less than 720 ships arriving in its harbour and departing with cargoes of timber and grain. Anglo-Danish relations needed to be good for English ships to navigate safely from the North Sea into the Baltic, thus the truce between the two nations in 1473 gave Lynn men easier access to the East.

Anglo-Prussian commerce post the Treaty of Utrecht was largely channelled through Lynn whose export trade had been to a great extent dependent on the Baltic since the late 14th century. A group or Hanse of town merchants who handled the traffic has been identified by Fudge. Particularly noteworthy is Robert Bees, who was apparently the only English trader in the eastern Baltic in 1475 and 1476, clearly in the vanguard of Lynn's drive to restart business with Danzig. He is listed as a mercer in the calendar of borough freemen (1473), apprenticed to Edward Hamond. Bees had several business partners. With Richard Peper he exported cloth from the Norfolk port in 1484 in a Hamburg cogge whose cargo partly belonged to Danzigers. Bees was one of three Lynn merchants and two from Danzig who exported cloth in 1487 in the vessel of a fellow townsman named John Brekersley. In 1490 and 1491 he was involved with other local merchants in the hire of Prussian ships to transport bulk cargoes from the Baltic to the Wash port. Bees, Peper, Wright, Tyge, Trewe, Brodbank, Harde, Wolle, Brekersley and William Amfles were all Lynn 'potentiores' in the forefront of Anglo-Hanseatic trade. It was surely William Amfles who developed the remarkably well preserved Hampton Court in Nelson Street when he inherited the property in 1482. A timber and brick street range containing shops was added to the existing 14th century merchant house; a brick warehouse parallel to the river at its western end had been erected around 1450. The merchant mark of William Amfles is carved in the right-hand spandrel of the front door frame. To identify individual goods these marks were needed on casks and bales when Lynn traders shared cargo space in ships sailing to the Low Countries or Danzig. Anglo-Hanseatic trade through Lynn in the 1480s and 1490s was conducted by Hamburg merchants and skippers as well as those from Danzig.

In the last quarter of the 15th century Hanseatic merchants concentrated their cloth exports in London at the expense of England's other east coast ports. Excluding the bursts of activity in 1488–9 and 1492–2, when an impressive number of cloths (777 and 480 respectively) were exported from Lynn by 'Hansards', their annual total of cloths despatched from the Wash port was only between 100 and 200 in these decades. Lynn's attraction for German traders was now less its supplies of cloth or other commodities and more the markets in the town and its region for Baltic goods. Imports of wax revived after 1474, but there was also an increase in a variety of consumer goods brought by Hanseatic cogges: haberdashery, purses, tiles, wooden platters, linen, furniture, gloves and counters for example. Lynn's hinterland included Cambridge, a commercial crossroads for a large part of East Anglia, with the city's river link to the Wash harbour of the utmost importance. Its colleges were regularly purchasing various goods arriving from Lynn by boat, including wax, fish, timber, furniture, cloth and, by 1550, Newcastle coal to replace the diminishing local reserves of firewood. Lynn was indeed the port for Stourbridge Fair which was England's greatest trading mart springing up every September by the Cam.

If 30 English ships could be found at any one time in Danzig in the 1440s, only 12 had arrived there between 1474 and 1477. Lynn's trade with Prussia continued in short booms and slumps into the 1490s. There was however an upturn at the commencement of the 16th century as the customs particulars for 1503–04 tell. Fudge concludes that the combined Baltic cargoes of German and English traders amounted to 55 percent of the town's total cloth export trade to highlight its Prussian connection. Of the Baltic goods unloaded at Lynn in 1503–04, Danzig chests appear on the list, along with rafters, eels and platters. The 15th century chest in the nave of King's Lynn Minster is almost certainly one of these Danzig chests in which luxury goods were stored on the voyage from East to West. There is no doubt that Lynn was 'the main link' to Danzig on England's east coast as the trade statistics show [Fudge: 158]. The Norfolk port was therefore playing a not inconsiderable part in Anglo-Hanseatic commerce beyond 1500, despite London's growing control of the nation's overseas trade.

Commercial intercourse between Lynn and Prussia continued through the reign of Henry VIII and Fudge describes this activity as 'a presence maintained' [Salman & Barrow:18]. By 1530 its Baltic trade was firmly in English hands with a local group or Hanse despatching a few vessels to Danzig most years: three in 1531, four in 1536, two in 1537, three in 1538, at least six in 1540, two in 1541 and three in 1542. Small amounts of cloth were augmented by rabbit pelts, lambfells, lead and sometimes Bay salt re-exported from the Wash harbour. Ships probably undertook the long voyage eastward together, departing Lynn in April or May, and returning from Danzig in July and August every year. Wax, pitch, tar, timber, chests, tables and fish were imported from the Baltic by the Norfolk men who on occasions hired Hanseatic bottoms. Amongst the dozen or more Lynn merchants and ship owners engaged in the Prussia trade was the widow Cecily Some who sent cloth to Danzig and the Low Countries as well as grain to Iceland.

VIII

Lynn's Hanse House is the sole surviving medieval trading post of the Hanseatic League in England. The street range in the foreground rebuilt about 1752. This aerial view shows its quadrangular character and extent by the Great Ouse.

Because of its association with the principal port towns of the German hanse — Danzig, Hamburg, Lübeck, Bremen and Stralsund — Lynn can be classified as one of its key foreign trading partners. Its geographical position on England's east coast and broad hinterland via the Great Ouse made it a premier destination for German kogges carrying Baltic goods before 1300. Lynn merchants were in the vanguard of English penetration of the eastern Baltic from the 1380s as the home cloth industry drove the search for new markets. By 1400 the Wash port had particularly close ties with Danzig, whose harbour looms large in European and Hanseatic history. Anglo-German economic rivalry sometimes erupted into violence and boycotts which undermined commerce, but both sides shared an interest in peace. English and Hanseatic towns invested much time and money in embassies and conferences to overcome damaging disputes and resume normal business. Lynn merchants were also councillors, mayors and envoys supported by their King in the quest to secure markets and benefit the national economy. The Hanseatic *kontor* established in Lynn in 1475 was welcomed by English and German merchants as a positive step to reconnect and restart money making!

Select Bibliography

Barrow, T. & Salmon, P. eds. *Britain and the Baltic* (University of Sunderland Press 2003).

Biernat, C. & Cieslak, E. *History of Gdansk* (Gdansk 1998).

Dollinger, P. *The German Hansa* (London 1970).

Friedland, K. & Richards, P. *Essays in Hanseatic History* (Dereham 2005).

Fudge, J. Cargoes, *Embargoes and Emissaries: The Commercial and Political Interactions of England and the German Hanse 1450—1510* (University of Toronto 1995).

Harrison, R. ed. *The Chancery Rolls in so far as they refer to King's Lynn: Volume VI, Richard II, 1377 to 1399* (King's Lynn 1999).

Keyser, E. *Die Baugeschichte der Stadt Danzig* (Köln 1972).

Lloyd, T.H. *England and the German Hanse 1157—1611* (Cambridge 1991).

Richards, P. *King's Lynn* (Chichester 1990).

Index